£3·60

LC

D1383685

ORAL FORMULAIC LANGUAGE
IN THE BIBLICAL PSALMS

NEAR AND MIDDLE EAST SERIES

Oral Formulaic Language in the Biblical Psalms

ROBERT C. CULLEY

UNIVERSITY OF TORONTO PRESS

To My Mother and Father

Preface

THE ORIGIN of this study and its development to the present form owe a great deal to the help, comments, suggestions, and advice of others. The original idea of examining the writings of the Old Testament for evidence of oral formulaic composition grew out of a number of conversations held a few years ago with a friend, Donald F. Chapin, now Associate Professor of English at the University of Alberta. He was at the time attending a seminar offered by Professor J. B. Bessinger in which, among other things, the oral style of Old English was being considered. In the course of these conversations I was introduced to the work of Milman Parry, A. B. Lord, and F. P. Magoun, Jr.

My first investigations of the Old Testament, begun while I was studying at the University of Bonn, were directed towards the prophetic writings, but the results were not encouraging. At this stage, I had the opportunity of discussing the matter briefly with Professor Martin Noth. It was on his suggestion that I turned to the biblical psalms, and I soon found that they presented very suitable material for the sort of study I had in mind. Shortly after this, Lord's book *The Singer of Tales* appeared, and it provided an invaluable guide on almost all aspects of oral formulaic composition.

The present form of this study is a revision of a doctoral dissertation presented to the Department of Near Eastern Studies of the University of Toronto. The dissertation was prepared in the light of the suggestions and criticism of the members of my committee at Toronto, who read an early draft, and especially my supervisor, Professor J. W. Wevers, who offered detailed comments at several stages of the writing.

This work has been published with the help of a grant from the Humanities Research Council of Canada using funds provided by the Canada Council, and with the aid of the Publications Fund of the

University of Toronto Press. For this assistance I am deeply grateful. The editorial staff of the University of Toronto Press has also made a significant contribution to the final stages of preparation.

Montreal, 1966   R.C.C.

Contents

ORAL FORMULAIC LANGUAGE IN THE BIBLICAL PSALMS

Introduction

THE STUDY of oral literature has attracted increasing interest in recent years. This attention is well deserved since oral literature by no means consists of crude attempts at art by primitives but embraces a rich and varied content of epic poems, songs, hymns, laments, and stories in prose of every description. Careful field studies have provided us with a great deal of information about how oral literature is composed and preserved so that now differences between oral and written literature may be delineated and explored with some measure of confidence. Furthermore, armed with a knowledge of characteristics of oral style, scholars have turned to texts such as Homer, *Beowulf*, and the *Chanson de Roland*, all of which may have come from an oral tradition, and have sought to determine to what extent they reflect oral style.

The subject of oral tradition has also been discussed by students of the Old Testament, and for good reason since it is quite possible that many of the texts that make up the Old Testament were composed and preserved for a time in an oral form. In general, however, the discussion has been carried on without reference to field studies, with the result that the term "oral tradition" has not been as carefully defined and the characteristics of oral style not as fully described as might be desired. In an earlier article, I suggested that terms used in the discussion of oral tradition, such as "oral composition" and "oral transmission," should be carefully defined and explained, especially since material is available from folklore studies to provide a sound basis for such a project.[1] The next step following the definition of terms and the listing of the characteristics of orally composed and transmitted literature would be to analyse appropriate sections of the Old Testament to see if characteristics similar to those already found in orally composed literature are present. The present study, in which

[1] "An Approach to the Problem of Oral Tradition," *Vetus Testamentum*, XIII (1963), 113–25.

certain stylistic features found in the Old Testament are examined in the light of what is known in general about oral style, is of this type. Only one group of Old Testament texts, the biblical psalms, will be discussed; and this will be done with reference to only one method of oral composition.

In the past much light has been shed on dark areas of the people of Israel and their literature by exploring parallel situations in the history of other peoples about whom more is known. When faced with an embarrassing lack of information about conditions prevailing at a given time, scholars have often sought to sketch in the background of the few and insufficient facts available by drawing an analogy from another historical situation that is more fully documented, and so more completely understood. An example of this is M. Noth's use of descriptions of tribal amphictyonies in Ancient Greece and Italy in his discussion of the association of the Twelve Tribes of Ancient Israel.[2] Another instance of this procedure is the analogy drawn by A. Alt in his study *Der Gott der Väter* between the nature of the religion of some Arabian and Aramaean peoples, as discerned in their inscriptions, and the nature of the religion of the Patriarchal period described in the Book of Genesis.[3] Furthermore, S. Mowinckel's use of analogies, especially from Babylon, in the exposition of his theory concerning an Israelite enthronement festival might also be mentioned in this regard.[4] This method is in principle quite sound, since very often the discovery of a parallel about which more is known offers the only hope of interpreting the meagre facts at our disposal. But the extent to which such a study succeeds depends upon a careful and judicious treatment of the evidence.

For this reason care and thoroughness have been the aim both in the treatment of the evidence from the biblical psalms and in the discussion of the particular method of oral composition concerned. This latter aspect is complicated by the fact that information has been drawn from a number of sources. Since the literature on oral composition may not be familiar to many scholars in the Old Testament field, a survey of the articles consulted has been added in an Appendix so that the basis for the description of oral devices and characteristics may be seen clearly and understood fully.

---

[2] *Das System der Zwölf Stämme Israels* ("Beiträge zur Wissenschaft vom Alten und Neuen Testament," IV. Folge, Heft 1 [Stuttgart: W. Kohlhammer, 1930]).

[3] "Beiträge zur Wissenschaft vom Alten und Neuen Testament," III. Folge, Heft 12 (Stuttgart: W. Kohlhammer, 1929); also in *Kleine Schriften zur Geschichte des Volkes Israel* (2nd ed. rev.; München: C. H. Beck'sche Verlagsbuchhandlung, 1959), vol. I, pp. 1–78.

[4] *Psalmenstudien II: Das Thronbesteigungsfest Jahwäs und der Ursprung der Eschatologie* ("Videnskapsselskapets Skrifter, II, Hist-Filos. Klasse," 1921, no. 6 [Kristiania: Jacob Dybwad, 1922]).

1

Oral Formulaic Composition

A SOCIETY in which there is no reading or writing, or in which these skills are not widely used, preserves its literature by oral tradition. In general terms this means that the method of transmitting literature from one generation to the next is by word of mouth. It should be added that the coming of writing to a society need not cause an immediate revolution, for the change from a completely oral society to a fully literate one may be slow.[1] There are degrees of literacy owing to the fact that the use of writing may be limited for various reasons.[2] For instance, writing may be confined to certain groups or classes of people who employ it for commerce, diplomatic correspondence, or government records. Also the use of writing may be restricted by the difficulty of learning and using a particular script. In addition, the widespread use of writing naturally depends upon the availability of writing materials in considerable quantity.

More specifically, oral transmission may occur either in a fixed form or in an unfixed form. For example, a recent investigator found two kinds of informants in Crete.[3] There were those who could recite from memory a fixed text of the songs they knew. But there were also those who performed traditional poems in a freer form rather than from a fixed text. These two forms need further consideration.

The fixed form of transmission needs little elaboration. It is accomplished by verbatim memorization. For example, before the

[1] See the discussion in B. Gerhardsson, *Memory and Manuscript* ("Acta Seminarii Neotestamentici Upsaliensis," no. 22 [Uppsala: Almqvist & Wiksells, 1961]), p. 123. For example, it took some time for people to become accustomed to reading silently. In classical and mediaeval times it was common for people to read manuscripts by pronouncing each word aloud. See the discussion of this in H. J. Chaytor, "Reading and Writing," *Explorations*, III (1954), 12; and Gerhardsson, *op. cit.*, p. 47.

[2] See the discussion of this subject in Sterling Dow, "Minoan Writing," *American Journal of Archaeology*, LVIII (1954), 110f.; see also H. M. and N. K. Chadwick, *The Growth of Literature* (3 vols.; Cambridge: University Press, 1932–40), III, 697.

[3] J. A. Notopoulos, "The Homeric Hymns as Oral Poetry: A Study of Post Homeric Oral Tradition," *American Journal of Philology*, LXXXIII (1962), 338f.

Mishnah was put into writing, the traditions contained in it were transmitted orally by the rabbis, who repeated them to their students until the latter knew them by heart.[4] In some cases transmission continues to be oral even when a fixed written text is in existence. Both the Qur'ān and the Vedas have been transmitted for centuries by memorization through oral repetition.[5] A further example of this sort of thing was reported in Crete. An illiterate old man more than ninety years of age could recite a poem over 10,000 lines long and was always found accurate when checked with a copy of the text.[6]

The unfixed form of transmission is essentially different from the fixed form. Although this freer form of transmission is used for both prose and poetry, it has been studied most thoroughly as it applies to poetry.[7] Thus what follows will concern only the transmission of poetry. Those who transmit poetry in this form are not reciters who have the ability to memorize and retain traditional texts accurately but are poets whose main talent is creating poetry. These oral poets have not committed to memory fixed texts of traditional poems; rather they have learned how to perform these poems by composing them again in each performance. The poets know the stock phrases and stereotyped expressions in which the traditional poems are expressed. They also know the stock scenes and descriptions of narrative poems and the traditional forms of laments and hymns. By creatively combining and adapting traditional material these artists recompose traditional poems in each performance. Consequently no two performances of the same poem are exactly alike. Transmission is accomplished by continual recomposition. The poem remains the same in general outline but varies in wording, since the poet is striving to produce a worthy version each time he performs. Furthermore, since these poets have a great wealth of ready-made language and traditional outlines of common types of poems, scenes, and descriptions, they are able not only to retell traditional poems but also to create new poems based on traditional forms. For example, they can compose a new lament to suit a particular occasion by using traditional outlines and traditional language. The method of composition em-

[4] Gerhardsson, *Memory and Manuscript*, pp. 130f.

[5] E. Nielsen, *Oral Tradition* ("Studies in Biblical Theology," no. 11 [London: S.C.M. Press, 1954]), pp. 21–24; W. F. Albright, *From the Stone Age to Christianity* (2nd ed.; New York: Doubleday, 1957), pp. 64f.; see also the anecdote about the Parsee priest related by N. S. Nyberg, *Studien zum Hoseabuche* ("Uppsala Universitets Årsskrift," 1935:6), pp. 7f.

[6] J. A. Notopoulos, "Homer, Hesiod and the Achaean Heritage of Oral Poetry," *Hesperia*, XXIX (1960), 193, n. 53. Oral transmission of this kind can vary in quality. With careless transmitters, errors can occur. See E. Littmann, "Abessinische und semitische Poesie," *Zeitschrift der Deutschen Morgenländischen Gesellschaft*, IX (1930), 213f.

[7] For a detailed discussion of the studies upon which the following is based, see the Appendix.

ployed by such poets is called the "formulaic technique of oral composition," because the main devices used in the process are certain kinds of stock phrases and adaptations of stock phrases called formulas and formulaic phrases respectively.[8]

There is no comprehensive, up-to-date work describing the formulaic technique of oral composition as it is found in different cultures and different types of poetry. The description of the foregoing paragraph is based upon a number of studies.[9] The most important of these are field studies made in three areas: (1) M. Parry and A. B. Lord have carried out, among the Serbocroatian people, the most careful and thorough study of oral narrative poetry yet made; (2) M. B. Emeneau has studied the songs of the Todas of South India; and (3) a number of investigations have been made of Russian oral narrative and ceremonial poetry. These field studies vary considerably in thoroughness and detail, although it appears that in each case the oral formulaic technique is the method of composition. For example, the work of Parry and Lord is by far the most detailed in its description of oral composition and the devices used by oral poets. Their study is limited, however, to long oral narrative poems. On the other hand, the Russian studies offer a less detailed description of oral composition and its devices. Yet the poems collected by Russian investigators are of a greater variety, ranging from long oral narratives to very short laments. In addition to these field studies another kind of investigation has been carried out. Scholars have analysed texts such as the epics of Homer and certain Anglo-Saxon poems for oral characteristics. These analyses are not of the same value as the field studies since there is no external evidence that the texts concerned actually were composed orally. Nevertheless, the results are significant and they serve to amplify and illustrate the field studies.[10]

---

[8] These devices and others will be described in considerable detail in the next chapter. Although the formulaic technique of oral composition is very common, it is not the only method of oral composition possible. There is some evidence that some oral poets compose their poems in private and formulate a fixed text in their mind before performing it. See A. Musil, *The Manners and Customs of the Rwala Bedouins* (New York: American Geographical Society, 1928), pp. 284f.; *idem, Arabia Petraea* (Vienna: Alfred Hoelder, 1908), III, 233; R. C. Thurnwald, *Profane Literature of the Buin, Solomon Islands* ("Yale University Publications in Anthropology," no. 8 [New Haven, 1936]), p. 6.

[9] The studies that follow have been described more fully in the Appendix.

[10] The studies of the formulaic technique of oral composition referred to here and in the Appendix have been applied to the Old Testament in an extensive way by only two scholars: S. Gevirtz, *Patterns in the Early Poetry of Israel* ("Studies in Ancient Oriental Civilization," no. 32 [Chicago: University Press, 1963]) and W. Whallon, "Formulaic Poetry in the Old Testament," *Comparative Literature*, XV (1963), 1–14. Some other biblical scholars have shown familiarity with the literature on oral composition. W. F. Albright mentioned Parry's work on Homer in one of his articles and went on to suggest that the poets of the Canaanite epics of Ugarit must have used a similar method of composition. He did not elaborate further. See his "Some Oriental Glosses on the Homeric Problem," *American Journal of Archaeology*, LIV (1950), 162. C. H. Lohr has discussed the matter of oral composition and referred to some of the

Not only do these field and textual studies provide us with a reasonably good understanding of the oral formulaic technique and its devices and characteristics, but they also reveal a very important fact. This technique is clearly a universal phenomenon in the sense that it is likely to be found wherever oral literature exists. It is not a method of composition limited to a single place or time; the technique has been found among peoples in widely separated geographical areas and in different historical periods. Nor is it limited to one kind of poetry. It has been used in composing and transmitting very short poems as well as very long ones. Moreover, it is possible that the unfixed form of oral transmission may be the more common. When discussing the fixed and unfixed forms of transmission at the end of their three-volume study of oral literature, the Chadwicks remarked: " . . . on the whole we must regard the free variety, which allows more or less scope for improvisation, as the normal form of oral tradition, and strict memorization as the exceptional."[11] Thus, on the basis of the Chadwicks' experience, one can expect to find the unfixed form far more often than the fixed form.

The use of the formulaic technique of oral composition in a tradition of poetry has interesting implications for the poets concerned and for the kind of poetry they produce. A few of these ramifications are worth considering.

Only poets with talent for composition and considerable practice in composing could excel at this technique. The best poems are to be heard in performances by the most gifted poets who have developed their gift through long practice. This is especially true of long narrative poems, which must be good enough to hold the interest of an audience for a considerable length of time.[12] On the other hand, it has been found that shorter poems, such as laments and songs, were composed in some societies by a high proportion of the population. For example, it is claimed that everyone among the Todas of South India could compose songs in a highly stereotyped diction.[13] Furthermore, collectors of Russian oral literature found that ordinary people

---

literature on the subject in an article on the Gospel of Matthew, "Oral Techniques in the Gospel of Matthew," *Catholic Biblical Quarterly*, XXIII (1961), 403–35. Finally, J. Blenkinsopp has discussed oral style in a study of the stories about Samson, "Structure and Style in Judges 13–16," *Journal of Biblical Literature*, LXXXII (1963), 65–76. He refers to the work of Parry and Lord in note 21 on p. 72. Curiously enough, he states that oral composition means that a "piece is *composed* orally and committed at once to memory, not just that it is composed for oral recitation," and suggests that this was demonstrated by the work of Parry and Lord.

[11] H. M. and N. K. Chadwick, *The Growth of Literature*, III, 868.

[12] See the description of a singer's training and development in A. B. Lord, *The Singer of Tales* ("Harvard Studies in Comparative Literature," no. 24 [Cambridge: Harvard University Press, 1960]), pp. 13ff.

[13] M. B. Emeneau, "Oral Poets of South India—The Todas," *Journal of American Folklore*, LXXI (1958), 318.

could compose laments for the dead, although it was usual to hire a professional for the occasion.[14] Nevertheless, among both the Todas and the Russians, the composer who cultivated his talent through practice gained the widest recognition and was usually called upon on important occasions. It was through these poets that the tradition was fostered and maintained.[15]

The oral poet is both a preserver of tradition and a creative artist. These forces are held in tension within him. Since oral composition normally occurs before a group of people, the immediate relationship between the artist and his audience sets limits on what the artist can do. If he wants to keep his audience, then he will have to present his poetry in a way that is acceptable and pleasing to his hearers. He cannot boldly innovate and depart radically from the traditional. In fact, it appears that most oral poets do not want to do so.[16] They share with their audience the sense of what is acceptable and what is not. They gain as much satisfaction from producing good versions of traditional poems as their listeners receive from hearing them. On the other hand, the oral poet is not just one who patches together bits and pieces of traditional material; rather he works creatively within traditional limits.[17] As will be seen in the next chapter, he can be creative to a surprisingly high degree in the way in which he varies his stock phrases or formulas and applies them to different situations. Furthermore, the themes and motifs of oral poetry are quite flexible as far as length and content are concerned. Good poets can demonstrate their skill and ability by the way in which they elaborate and ornament the themes and motifs of the traditional poems.

In view of what we know about the formulaic technique of oral composition, it is quite inaccurate to speak of "author" and of "original text," at least within the connotations that these terms have in a literary society. Lord makes this point very well with reference to the oral narrative tradition.[18] In a sense the performer is the author, but only in terms of a particular performance. A good performance is the result of a skilful and talented poet working with traditional language and themes that have been produced by many poets over many years. Likewise, there can be no "original text." On the contrary, a song is much more likely to be performed well after it has been performed many times.[19]

---

[14] Y. M. Sokolov, *Russian Folklore*, trans. C. R. Smith (New York: Macmillan, 1950), pp. 226, 229.

[15] H. M. and N. K. Chadwick, *The Growth of Literature*, II, 286.

[16] Lord, *Singer of Tales*, pp. 4ff., 28f., 102.

[17] For what follows, see A. B. Lord, "Homer's Originality: Oral Dictated Texts," *Transactions and Proceedings of the American Philological Association*, LXXXIV (1953), 127f.

[18] For what follows, see *Singer of Tales*, pp. 100ff.

[19] *Ibid.*, p. 100.

2

The Devices and Characteristics of Oral Formulaic Composition

ALTHOUGH it is true that the investigation of oral style and oral poets still continues and that our knowledge of these matters is still incomplete, a great deal can be said at this stage about devices and characteristics. The devices usually mentioned in discussions of oral formulaic composition are the formula and the theme. The formula, however, is the important device as far as the biblical psalms are concerned, but even the study of this device alone requires a rather extended discussion.

FORMULAS AND FORMULAIC SYSTEMS

A formula in oral poetry is a repeated group of words the length of which corresponds to one of the divisions in the poetic structure, such as the line or the smaller divisions within the line created by some formal division such as the caesura. Formulas are used repeatedly by oral poets because they are useful, in fact necessary, for rapid oral composition. When an oral poet is composing during a performance, he does not have time to experiment with combinations of words until he finds just the right one that will express what he wants to say and at the same time fit the metrical structure of his poetry. Formulas provide him with ready-made phrases in suitable metrical form for the ideas he wants to use in his poems.

The usefulness of formulas in composition is seen in a number of ways. The fact that the same phrase is employed by a poet a great many times is some indication at least that it is useful to him in some way.[1] A clearer indication of the usefulness of formulas for composition is seen in their structure. The fact that the length of formulas

[1] M. Parry, "Studies in the Epic Technique of Oral Verse-Making. I: Homer and Homeric Style," *Harvard Studies in Classical Philology*, XLI (1930), 81.

corresponds to the divisions of the poetry in which they are found shows that the formulas are in a usable form and can be fitted into poetic structure quite easily.[2] Finally, the best illustration of the usefulness of formulas is the formulaic system. A full description of this and how it shows the usefulness of formulas will be given below.

The definition of the formula just given differs from the widely accepted definition given by Parry. He defined the formula in the Homeric poems as "a group of words which is regularly employed under the same metrical conditions to express a given essential idea."[3] He wished to draw attention to what he considered to be the essential characteristic of a formula, namely, its usefulness in oral composition. This important point is also implied in the definition given above. But Parry's definition suffers from the drawback that it describes the usefulness of the formula in terms of a feature of Homer which Parry called "thrift." In the Homeric poems one formula is regularly used to express one idea under the same metrical conditions.[4] Alternative formulas expressing the same idea and having the same metrical value are not common. Parry thought that this was a significant sign of oral composition since it showed that the poet always used the same expression for a given idea rather than inventing synonymous expressions as he might have done. Further study, however, has shown that the principle of thrift is valid only under certain conditions. Lord reports that thrift is significant when the works of one singer are being considered but far less significant, if at all, when a tradition is being studied.[5] F. P. Magoun, Jr., comments that the degree of thrift found in Greek epic poetry is not possible in the verse form of Germanic poetry, which is more restrictive because of the use of alliteration.[6] Thus, Parry's definition could be misleading when applied to poetry other than Homer.

The working definition of the formula given above is expressed in general terms so that it can be widely applied. When the formula is defined with respect to any one tradition, further qualifications and explanations may be added. We have already seen that the definition of the formula in the Homeric poems can be modified to include

[2] See A. B. Lord, "Homer and Other Epic Poetry," in *A Companion to Homer*, eds. A. J. B. Wace and F. H. Stubbings (London: Macmillan, 1962), pp. 186ff. In this article Lord outlines the formula structure of a number of oral traditions. For example, he points out that the line of Serbocroatian epic poetry is ten syllables long with a break coming regularly after the fourth syllable. Thus, the formulas of this poetry would be ten, six, and four syllables in length. These lengths correspond to the natural divisions of the poetry, the line and the parts of the line formed by the caesura.

[3] "Studies I," p. 80.

[4] *Ibid.*, p. 86.

[5] *The Singer of Tales* ("Harvard Studies in Comparative Literature," no. 24 [Cambridge: Harvard University Press, 1960]), p. 53.

[6] "Oral-Formulaic Character of Anglo-Saxon Narrative Poetry," *Speculum*, XXVIII (1953), 450.

the notion of thrift. For Old English poetry Magoun would change the first part of Parry's definition to read "a word or group of words."[7] It is Magoun's view that a formula in Anglo-Saxon poetry can be a single word, since the verse and the two measures making up the verse may be quite short.

Strictly speaking, repetition of a formula should be exact. But since it is essentially the metrical value of formulas that makes them useful to the oral poet, scholars have permitted certain modifications within the formula as long as this metrical value is not thereby changed. Parry allowed changes of inflectional endings and the addition or omission of small particles.[8] Because of the strict metre of Greek epic poetry, any changes beyond these would alter the metrical form. On the other hand, Anglo-Saxon poetry permits considerable variation in the number of syllables in a verse and so changes of gender, number case, tense, and mood can occur without altering the metrical structure. Consequently, such variations have been permitted to formulas in Anglo-Saxon.[9]

Closely related to the formula is the formulaic system. A formulaic system may be described as a group of phrases having the same syntactical pattern, the same metrical structure, and at least one major lexical item in common. The following is an example from Southslavic poetry:[10]

		nahod Simeune
		(the foundling Simeon)
	njemu (to him)	Todore vezire
		(Theodore the high counsellor)
veli (said)	njojzi (to her)	Miloš čobanine
		(Milosh the Shepherd)
	njima (to them)	srpski car Stjepane
		(the Serbian emperor Stephen)
		kraljeviću Marko
		(the king's son Mark)

This system contains five standard epic lines of ten syllables. These five lines have the same syntactic pattern: verb, pronoun, proper noun with one or more modifiers. The verb has two syllables, the pronouns all have two syllables, and the last part of the line has six syllables. The verb is the constant lexical item. Thus, the pattern of this formulaic system is:

veli + pronoun (2 syllables) + noun and modifier(s) (6 syllables).

[7] "The Theme of the Beasts of Battle in Anglo-Saxon Poetry," *Neuphilologische Mitteilungen*, LVI (1955), 81.
[8] "Studies I," p. 83.
[9] R. Diamond, "The Diction of the Signed Poems of Cynewulf," *Philological Quarterly*, XXXVIII (1959), 230.
[10] M. Parry, "Whole Formulaic Verses in Greek and Southslavic Heroic Songs," *Transactions and Proceedings of the American Philological Association*, LXIV (1933), 184.

The same pattern can be adapted to different contexts by substitution of different lexical items having the same number of vowels. In this way, the metrical structure and thereby the usefulness of the pattern are preserved. Like formulas, the patterns of formulaic systems are of the same length as the divisions of the poetic structure, such as lines and the parts of the lines created by some formal division such as the caesura. Practical reasons dictate the insistence upon one common lexical item. Only in this way can it be demonstrated with some assurance that phrases with the same syntactical pattern and the same metrical values are actually variations of a single pattern.[11]

Phrases that make up a formulaic system may be of two kinds. There may be phrases that appear a number of times and so are formulas in their own right. On the other hand, there may be phrases that occur only once in the material under study and so cannot be shown to be formulas. The latter phrases will be called "formulaic phrases," since they share a syntactic pattern, a metrical pattern, and one lexical item with other phrases.[12]

It has already been suggested that the existence of formulaic systems best illustrates the fact that formulas are functional. Parry had noticed that the formulas of the Homeric poems could be arranged in systems of considerable length and complexity. Lord claims that the establishment of patterns that can easily be modified by substitution to express what a poet wishes to say is the heart of the formulaic technique of oral composition.[13] The poet, in memorizing a great many formulas to cover every situation, has thereby also learned patterns with which he can create new formulas and formulaic phrases by analogy. Lord also draws attention to the fact that this method of oral composition is analogous to what occurs in language learning in general. Phrases and sentences are constructed by substitution within the syntactic patterns of a language. Formulas in oral poetry provide the patterns

[11] See M. Parry, "Studies I," p. 85. Parry's definition of a formulaic system is as follows: "a group of phrases which have the same metrical value and which are enough alike in thought and words to leave no doubt that the poet who used them knew them not only as a single formula but also as formulas of a certain type." He limited membership in a system to phrases "in which not only the metre and the parts of speech are the same, but in which also at least one important word or group of words is identical." Parry's definition implies that all the phrases in a system were formulas but he recognizes elsewhere (p. 117) that some need not be. For Magoun's discussion of systems, see "Oral-Formulaic Character . . .," p. 449.

[12] Lord, *Singer of Tales*, p. 47.

[13] *Ibid.*, p. 37. See also A. Schmaus, "Formel und metrisch-syntaktisches Modell," *Die Welt der Slaven*, V (1960), 395–408. Schmaus also recognizes the important role of patterns in an epic tradition: "Jene Tradition lebt nur zum geringeren Teil in den fertigen Formeln; ihre eigentliche Macht wirkt über den 'epischen Wortschatz' hinaus und durch ihn hindurch als ein sehr differenziertes und fein verästeltes im Mühen vieler Generationen aus den Potenzen der Sprache gewonnenes und in immer neuen Realisierungen erprobtes und bewährtes System metrisch-syntaktischer Modelle" (p. 408).

within which substitution may occur. This living and creative process has been described by Lord in the following way: "If the oral poet is never at a loss for a word or a group of words to express his idea, it is because the formulaic technique has provided him not with the formula for every idea, but with a means of constantly recomposing the formulae for the less common ideas, with a sufficient variety of patterns so that the idea can take almost instantaneous form in the rhythm of his song."[14]

The use of formulas and formulaic phrases leaves its mark on poetry created in this way. The effect the formulaic technique of oral composition has on poetic style shows itself in a number of ways, three of which might be mentioned.

In the first place, groups of formulas and formulaic phrases, amounting sometimes to several lines, occasionally recur a number of times in the same or slightly different order. Lord calls such a recurring group of lines a "run" or a "cluster."[15] He suggests that this phenomenon is the result of the formulaic method of composition. As a poet repeats his songs, the same lines containing the same formulas are repeated often in the same contexts. These groups of formulas thus become associated in the poet's mind and tend to be repeated in the same or slightly altered form.

Secondly, much oral poetry is composed in what Parry has called an "adding style."[16] By this he meant that the unit of composition is usually the single line and that a poem is made by line being added to line. Regular stanzas are rare. The line generally corresponds to a syntactic structural unit in that the end of a line coincides with a natural break such as the end of a sentence or clause. In other words, enjambment is not common in oral poetry.[17] The frequency of occurrence of enjambment is so much lower in oral poetry than in written that some would make its absence one of the tests for oral style.[18]

Finally, composition by formulas and formulaic phrases has led at times to some curious inconsistencies and contradictions. Through force of habit, the poet is not always careful to adjust the traditional formulas he is using to the subject at hand. This sort of thing has been found in noun-adjective combinations in which the adjective is not appropriate to the noun. For example, C. M. Bowra cites a case

---

[14] "Homer and Other Epic Poetry," p. 188.
[15] *Singer of Tales*, p. 58.
[16] *Ibid.*, p. 54.
[17] *Ibid.* See also, p. 284, n. 17. Here Lord distinguishes between unperiodic and necessary enjambment. According to him, a line may end in one of three ways: (1) by the end of a sentence; (2) by the end of a word group so that the thought ends, although the sentence goes on (non-periodic enjambment); and (3) by a break in the middle of a word group (necessary enjambment). In oral poetry, it is the last kind, necessary enjambment, that is not common.
[18] *Ibid.*, p. 145.

in which the commonly used adjective "fair-haired" has been applied to a Moor.[19] J. Ross provides a further example from Gaelic poetry in the phrase "brown haired girl of the fair hair."[20] In both of these an adjective has been used, likely through habit, with a noun to which it does not apply. Little systematic investigation has been made of possible inconsistencies resulting from the formulaic technique. But anyone dealing with oral poetry or texts having oral characteristics should be aware that such things can and do happen.

Most formulas and patterns of formulaic systems are traditional. They have been handed down through the years by successive generations of singers, and are the common property of a number of singers at any one time. Under this general subject of traditional formulas a number of observations can be drawn together.

The sound of words and phrases is of particular importance in oral poetry.[21] Oral poets are undoubtedly sensitive to the patterns of sounds in the words and phrases they use. There is some evidence that the sound patterns of formulas and groups of formulas are used by poets to heighten the total effect of their poetry on the listeners. Lord has shown how Serbocroatian poets used such devices as internal rhyme, chiastic arrangement of consonants, and repetition of vowel patterns to create such an effect. This matter of sound patterns is related to the subject of traditional formulas in an important way. Lord claims that formulaic lines containing striking arrangements of consonants and vowels persist for quite a long time.

Since many formulas continue to be in use in a tradition for long periods of time, it follows that many would contain a great deal of matter from earlier days. Some of this would be archaic words, phrases, and ideas.[22] Bowra found that formulas "preserve relics of lost beliefs and outmoded theological ideas."[23] Foreign elements have also been found preserved in formulas,[24] which may be a reflection of the time when poets moved from place to place or when poetic traditions of one people mingled with the poetic traditions of another.[25]

---

[19] *Heroic Poetry* (London: Macmillan, 1952), p. 239. See also Y. M. Sokolov, *Russian Folklore*, trans. C. R. Smith (New York: Macmillan, 1950), p. 307.

[20] "Formulaic Composition in Gaelic Oral Literature," *Modern Philology*, LVII (1959), 3.

[21] *Lord, Singer of Tales*, p. 56.

[22] M. Parry, "Studies in the Epic Technique of Oral Verse-Making. II: The Homeric Language as the Language of an Oral Poetry," *Harvard Studies in Classical Philology*, XLIII (1932), 10ff. See also H. M. and N. K. Chadwick, *The Growth of Literature* (3 vols.; Cambridge: University Press, 1932–40), II, 122. Here these writers claim that "the use of obsolete words also suggests that the *byliny* have retained traces of some earlier actual milieu."

[23] *Heroic Poetry*, p. 397.

[24] M. Parry, "Studies II," pp. 11ff.

[25] M. B. Emeneau, "Oral Poets of South India—The Todas," *Journal of American Folklore*, LXXI (1958), 320. Emeneau points out that the poetic language of the Todas was different from the language of everyday life. He says that this difference was largely

On the other hand, because new formulas were continually being made on the analogy of the old, new formulas might be made on archaic or foreign patterns so that peculiar mixtures of old and new come into existence. Parry's warning is surely pertinent at this point: "a word, form, or group of words which is old or foreign is not in itself proof that the verse or passage in which it is found is the work of an older or foreign singer."[26]

If most formulas have been passed on for some time and are also the property of a number of singers or poets at any given time, then we may speak of a common stock of traditional formulas. Lord provides a good discussion on this subject.[27] The common stock of a poetic tradition would contain every formula used by more than one poet. Most common formulas would be used by quite a number of poets at the same time and some would be used by all. Distinctions can be made within the common stock of a poetic tradition. There is the stock of a single poet consisting of all the formulas he knows and uses. This would contain largely formulas learned from others, i.e., some but not all of those in the common stock, as well as those created by the poet himself. The stock of a single poet is never exactly identical with the common stock or with the stock of any other poet. Furthermore, one may speak of the stock of a group of poets, such as those in a particular area or district. As a further step, the common stock of the poets in a group of districts could be considered. This process of enlarging the area of investigation can be continued until all the poets in a tradition are included.[28] It should be emphasized, however, that the common stock of a tradition is not static. The tradition is living since the stocks of individual poets are always being enlarged as they learn more traditional formulas and create new ones of their own. The most widely used formulas of the traditional stock will be those formulas dealing with the ideas and actions that occur most often in the poetry concerned. For instance, Lord points out that the most stable formulas of Serbocroatian oral narrative poetry are those containing the names of the actors, those expressing the main actions, and those that are expressions of time and place.[29]

Each different kind of poetry has its own common stock of traditional language. Parry claimed that in Yugoslav poetry "traditional dictions

---

due to archaisms and borrowings from neighbours. He hesitates to claim, however that the presence of these elements was necessarily due either completely or in part to the fact that the poetry was oral.

[26] "Studies II," p. 23.

[27] What follows is based on the discussion in Lord, *Singer of Tales*, pp. 49f.

[28] *Ibid.*, p. 49. Lord suggests that the study of a common stock must begin where possible with the stock of a single singer, then move on to the stock of his district, and, proceeding through ever larger groups, come finally to the whole tradition.

[29] *Ibid.*, pp. 34ff.

can exist side by side for different verse-forms and for different types of poetry."[30] A different subject matter means that different formulas are needed. As we have seen, the most common formulas in a tradition are expressions of the actions and subjects most often handled in the poetry of that tradition. For example, narrative poetry would have one body of traditional language, songs another, and laments another. There might be overlapping where subjects were common, but by and large each kind of poetry would have its own traditional stock.

One final observation on traditional language can be made. Traditional language can survive a considerable change in the society or culture in which the oral literature is at home. Two examples may be cited. We are told that after the change from paganism to Christianity Anglo-Saxon singers were able to adapt with only slight adjustments the traditional language of pagan times to Christian themes.[31] A second example comes from studies made of a well-known Russian singer. These studies show how she adapted traditional language to new themes.[32] This singer knew many of the old, traditional narrative songs and could sing them very well. After the revolution, however, she began to compose songs on Soviet themes. One of the most famous of these is a lament for Lenin. Although these new songs deal with new conditions of society and culture, they are to a large extent expressed in the traditional language of the old songs.

THE THEME

The next device to be considered is the theme. Whether this device appears in the biblical psalms or not is by no means clear. Nevertheless, a full understanding of formulaic composition requires a knowledge of it. As a compositional device, the theme is essentially different from the formula. The formula has to do with formal characteristics of lines and parts of lines such as the patterns of syntax and metre. The theme has to do with content, i.e., with elements of subject matter, in groups of lines that have no fixed form. A theme is a "recurrent element of narration or description in traditional oral poetry."[33] It is a typical scene or stock description. A common theme in Serbocroatian oral narrative is that of the gathering of an army.[34]

---

[30] "Studies I," p. 92.
[31] F. P. Magoun, Jr., "Oral-Formulaic Character . . .," p. 457.
[32] Sokolov, *Russian Folklore*, pp. 671ff.; C. M. Bowra, *Heroic Poetry*, pp. 469ff.; K. Hartmann, "Die Rhapsodin M. S. Krjukova, ihre sowjetischen Volkspoeme und deren Verhältnis zur Tradition des grossrussischen Heldenliedes," *Die Welt der Slaven*, II (1957), 394–418.
[33] A. B. Lord, "Composition by Theme in Homer and Southslavic Epos," *Transactions and Proceedings of the American Philological Association*, LXXXII (1951), 73.
[34] *Singer of Tales*, p. 68.

The elements of this theme, as described by Lord, are: the chieftain writes letters to other chiefs, preparations are made for their reception, and the groups are described as they arrive. A theme can vary greatly in length: it can be described quite fully and elaborately or very briefly in a few lines. The theme aids the poet in a similar way as the formula does, only on a larger scale. Just as formulas and patterns of formulaic systems provide the poet with ready-made phrases, so themes provide the poet with ready-made scenes and descriptions.[35] Finally, we can speak of a stock of traditional themes, just as we could speak of a stock of traditional formulas. Poets use formulas to build lines, lines are added to one another to fill out the frameworks of themes, and themes are added one to another to tell the story of the particular poem being narrated.

It may be that some further refinements will be made in the definition and description of the theme. Lord claims that the units Anglo-Saxon scholars have been calling themes are not really themes but rather motifs. Examples of this may be found in a discussion of the beasts of battle theme in Anglo-Saxon poetry by Magoun.[36] He presents twelve passages, from three to eighteen verses long, which he claims are examples of this theme. It consists of the mentioning of three creatures—the raven, the eagle, and the wolf—in connection with a battle. Four of the twelve passages mention all three creatures and most of the other passages mention at least two of them. This sort of thing is a much smaller unit both in length and structure than the unit suggested by Lord's discussion of theme. Thus, scholars may eventually agree in distinguishing between theme and motif. At any rate, the nature of theme as understood by Lord and theme as understood by Magoun is essentially the same: a group of ideas recurring in a variable form.

Up to this point the theme has been discussed only with reference to oral narrative poetry. There is no reason, however, why similar repeated groups of ideas or elements could not be devices in other kinds of oral poetry as well.[37] For instance, elegies and some kinds of ceremonial poetry in Russian oral literature have certain elements of content which continually reappear over long periods of time in successive examples of the same type. The Chadwicks claim that "what might almost be called the Platonic 'idea' of a given type of poem survives from generation to generation."[38] A good example of this is the type referred to as the lament of the troops on the death

---

[35] Magoun, "The Theme of the Beasts of Battle . . .," p. 83.
[36] *Ibid.*, pp. 81ff.
[37] Lord mentions the existence of themes in folktales and myths. See *Singer of Tales*, p. 284, n. 1.
[38] *Growth of Literature*, II, 286.

of a sovereign.[39] The constant elements in these laments are: (1) an opening, which is a brief address to some natural object such as the moon; (2) a description of the body of the sovereign lying in state with a soldier standing guard; and (3) a speech made by the soldier. Here is a repeated group of elements in a variable form. This is how a theme was defined. Thus, where repeated groups of ideas are found in short poems, the question should be raised as to whether this might be a compositional device similar to that of the theme in oral narrative.

OTHER DEFINITIONS OF THE FORMULA AND THE THEME

The working definitions for the formula, the formulaic system, and the theme given in the preceding paragraphs have been based on the work of Parry and Lord and other scholars who have followed their methods. Not all students of oral literature, however, have defined these characteristics in the same way or with the same terminology. For instance, when Sokolov speaks of traditional formulas in Russian literature, he means typical scenes and episodes such as the saddling of a horse or the arrival of someone at court.[40] The work of two scholars, C. M. Bowra and J. Ross, calls for comment in this regard.

Bowra uses only the one term "formula" and gives it a broad definition.[41] He speaks of three classes of formulas: (1) the short formula, which is a noun-adjective combination; (2) the repeated line; and (3) the repeated theme. Two objections can be raised against this definition. In the first place, a distinction is made by Bowra which is not necessary. The short formula and the repeated line need not be separated since they are of the same order. Once it is stated that formulas conform to the natural division of the poetry such as the line and the divisions within the line, there is no need to distinguish between longer and shorter formulas. A second and more serious objection is that Bowra fails to make an important distinction. The formula and theme do not belong in the same category, since the former has to do principally with form and the latter with content. Consequently, these two devices should be defined separately and not taken as subclasses of a single device.

Another proposal to give the term "formula" a broader definition

---

[39] N. K. Chadwick, *Russian Heroic Poetry* (Cambridge: University Press, 1932). See the poems on pp. 210, 274, 284, and 290. These are the laments for Ivan the Terrible, Peter the Great, Empress Katherine II, and Tzar Alexander I, thus spanning a long period of history. These poems vary from twenty to fifty lines in length. Even in the English translation the similarities and differences in language and structure can be seen.

[40] *Russian Folklore*, p. 305.

[41] "Style," in *A Companion to Homer*, eds. A. J. B. Wace and F. H. Stubbings (London: Macmillan, 1962), pp. 26ff.

has come from the study of Gaelic poetry. J. Ross argues that Parry's definition must be expanded.[42] Ross agrees that there are exact repetitions but he also claims that there are "conceptual formulas." These are defined as "recurrent ideas in different metrical contexts."[43] He means ideas that appear a number of times but in a different wording and a different metrical form in each case. He gives examples of ideas recurring in a single-line form, a couplet form, and larger groups of lines. The objection must also be raised here that this definition confuses two different things: the formula, which has a fixed form, and the theme or motif, which has a variable form. If what Ross calls "conceptual formulas" are indeed a device of oral composition, they would be discussed more profitably in connection with the theme and the motif, since they involve repeated subject matter rather than form. Incidentally, Ross's examples come from a tradition of oral composition that is no longer living, and so there appears to be no way of discovering how individual singers employed recurrent ideas in a line or two-line form. Further investigations will have to be made in different kinds of oral literature to see how common such a device of composition might be.

[42] "Formulaic Composition . . .," pp. 1–12.
[43] *Ibid.*, p. 4.

3

Oral Formulaic Composition and Texts

ORAL CHARACTERISTICS have been studied in two classes of texts. Texts of the first class are those collected in field studies and recorded by machine or by dictation from the lips of oral performers. Along with these texts, the collectors have usually supplied a description of the method of composition used by the poets concerned and the means used to record their works. In other words, we know how these texts originated. The same cannot be said, however, for the second class of texts, such as the Homeric poems and *Beowulf*, which have come down to us in a written form, but about the origin of which we know very little. For these poems, and others like them, there is no description whatsoever of how they were composed or put into writing. This class of texts, then, raises an important question: if oral characteristics are present in a text, is it correct to conclude that such a text is a record of an oral performance? Or to put it another way, does the presence of formulas and formulaic phrases always indicate oral composition?

This question is not easily answered and it opens up a very complex matter, of which three areas call for close examination. In the first place, it is necessary to understand clearly what the normal level of formulaic content is in orally composed poetry and how the level can be established in texts. Then, too, the possible methods of recording texts ought to be reviewed and evaluated to see how accurate a reproduction these different methods yield. Finally, the question of a mixture of oral and literary style must be broached.

How pervasive are formulas and formulaic phrases in orally composed poetry? Lord contends that the greater part of an orally composed poem will consist of formulas and formulaic phrases and that the amount of non-formulaic material will be small. A literary text, on the contrary, will show just the reverse.[1] Although oral texts

[1] A. B. Lord, *The Singer of Tales* ("Harvard Studies in Comparative Literature," no. 24 [Cambridge: Harvard University Press, 1960]), p. 130; see also F. P. Magoun, Jr., "Oral-Formulaic Character of Anglo-Saxon Narrative Poetry," *Speculum*, XXVIII (1953), 447; C. M. Bowra, *Heroic Poetry* (London: Macmillan, 1952), p. 93.

are predominantly formulaic, the texts of the most talented singers will likely contain the highest amounts of non-formulaic material. There is good reason for this. Those who have mastered their art are not the prisoners of their method. As a consequence, gifted singers are able to break away from formulaic language more often than the less gifted.[2] But even in such cases the formulaic content is far higher than in normal literary texts. Thus, it would seem that the amount of formulas and formulaic phrases in a text provides a ready indicator of whether a text is an oral or literary composition.

It is not always easy to establish, however, the exact content of formulas and formulaic phrases in a poem, since everything depends on the total amount of material available for study. Phrases can only be shown to be formulas when they recur at least once, preferably several times, in a body of material. Likewise, phrases can only be shown to be formulaic phrases when they can be placed with another phrase, or preferably several other phrases, to form a system with a common pattern. Thus, the larger the body of material, the greater is the chance of finding phrases repeated and of identifying them as formulaic language. In some cases the material is so extensive that no serious problem arises. There are often several thousand lines from the same singer available in the collections of Parry and Lord. A sample passage from Serbocroatian oral narrative could be shown to be entirely formulaic.[3] Homer also contains a great deal of material, over 27,000 lines.[4] Consequently it should not be difficult to establish a considerable amount of formulaic language. But as the body of material available for comparison decreases, so does the likelihood of showing lines and half-lines to be formulas and formulaic phrases.

In view of this, it is evident that the amount of formulaic and non-formulaic material can only be discussed in relative terms. The percentage of formulaic material that can be established in a poem may represent only part of the true figure, if the total body of poetry being studied is small. Likewise, it cannot be said with regard to the remaining material that it is definitely non-formulaic, because the availability of more material for comparison might result in the establishing of more formulas and formulaic phrases. Thus, when referring to language that cannot be proved to be formulaic, it is preferable to label it as "non-formulaic with respect . . . to the quantity of material used in analysis."[5] As a consequence of all this, no percentage can be set which could then be used as a measuring stick to decide whether a text is an oral composition or not.

[2] Lord, *Singer of Tales*, p. 131; Bowra, *Heroic Poetry*, p. 252.
[3] Lord, *Singer of Tales*, p. 46.
[4] *Ibid.*, pp. 158ff.
[5] Lord as quoted in W. A. O'Neil, "Another Look at Oral Poetry in *The Seafarer*," *Speculum*, XXXV (1960), 599.

In addition to the fact that percentages are only relative, there is another problem. While Lord is essentially correct in pointing out that oral texts will have a high formulaic content and literary texts will have a low formulaic content, there are occasions, as will be seen, when the line between the two is blurred. Here again no general rule can be laid down; rather the significance of a percentage must be gauged in each case separately.

We move on now to the next matter to be discussed: how orally composed poems are recorded. What are the ways in which an orally composed poem might find its way into writing and how accurately would the resulting texts reflect an oral performance? In modern field studies oral poetry may be recorded mechanically so that the text produced is simply a transcript of an oral performance. While it is irrelevant to discuss this method of recording with regard to earlier texts, it is, as will be seen, the only method that yields a completely accurate reproduction of an oral performance. The remaining means of recording texts must now be considered in some detail.

Perhaps the most obvious method of recording a text is by dictation. It has been found, however, that dictated texts of oral narrative poems differ from oral performances. Oral poets using the oral formulaic technique produce a different kind of text when dictating than when singing before an audience under normal conditions.[6] The difference is due to a number of things. In a normal performance the poet sings or recites his poem before an audience, whereas for dictation he must recite very slowly and so the usual rhythm and movement of the poem are lacking as well as the inspiration provided by an attentive audience. Furthermore, a singer who is accustomed to singing his songs has considerable difficulty in adapting himself to slow recitation. This difficulty is in turn reflected in his style, which may betray variations in line structure as well as a less consistent use of poetic devices than a normal oral performance.[7] Over against these disadvantages of dictated texts, there is one distinct advantage, which has been noticed by Lord. When a poet is given an unlimited amount of time to dictate, he tends to elaborate far more than usual so that he produces a much longer and richer poem than he would

---

[6] For what follows, see A. B. Lord, "Homer's Originality: Oral Dictated Texts," *Transactions and Proceedings of the American Philological Association*, LXXXIV (1953), 124–34; *idem, Singer of Tales*, pp. 127ff.; *idem.* (ed.), *Serbocroatian Heroic Songs, Vol. I: Novi Pazar: English Translations*, collected by Milman Parry and edited and translated by A. B. Lord (Cambridge: Harvard University Press, 1954), pp. 7f.; H. M. and N. K. Chadwick, *The Growth of Literature* (3 vols.; Cambridge: University Press, 1932–40), III, 179ff.

[7] R. Austerlitz, "Ob-Ugric Metrics," *FF Communications*, 174 (1958), 13f.; Lord, *Singer of Tales*, p. 126.

in a performance. Lord maintains that dictated songs are the best.[8]
He quotes a dictum of some of Parry's Serbocroatian singers: "sung
songs are truer, dictated songs are finer."[9]

Then too, oral poets who are literate can write down their own
texts. This process is similar to dictation since the oral poet dictates
to himself in much the same way as he would dictate to another.[10]
But Lord contends on the basis of his own experience that a text
written down by the poet himself was inferior to a text dictated to
another.[11] One would have appreciated a fuller exposition of this point
on Lord's part. It is to be hoped that more information will be
forthcoming not only from Lord but from other investigators as well
to see whether it can be taken as a general rule that texts transcribed
by an oral poet himself are of poor quality.

There is a third possibility that ought to be considered, although
it has not been studied fully or discussed. Both of the preceding
methods of dictation involve the copying down of a work that is being
produced by the oral formulaic technique during the act of dictation.
In such a case the recording takes place while the technique of oral
formulaic composition is still alive and flourishing. But might there
not be a gap between the period of flourishing oral composition and
the time of recording? That is, is it not possible that poems trans-
mitted in a relatively unfixed form by means of the oral formulaic
technique could attain a fixed form and then be passed on by
memorization until written down? A hint that this may be possible
is given in the Chadwicks' description of the transmission of the
Vedas.[12] They suggest that the earliest transmission of the hymns
of the Rigveda was rather free. Another scholar, Emeneau, suggests
that the oral formulaic technique was actually used in the composition
of these hymns.[13] This method came to an end with the fixation of
the oral text, which apparently occurred some time before a written
text was created. If such a process is possible, then dictation would
simply involve the recitation to a scribe of a memorized, fixed oral
poem. Since composition is not taking place during dictation, the
style of the poem would not be affected by the slower performance.
Much of this, however, remains a matter of speculation at present.
A great deal of further investigation must be carried on before it is

---

[8] Lord, *Singer of Tales*, p. 128. Lord distinguishes further between good and bad
recording. A skilful, patient scribe can elicit the best from a singer. See p. 149.
[9] "Homer's Originality," p. 131.
[10] R. Austerlitz, "Ob-Ugric Metrics," p. 13, n. 5.
[11] *Singer of Tales*, pp. 129, 149.
[12] *Growth of Literature*, II, 462f., 595, 602.
[13] "Oral Poets of South India—The Todas," *Journal of American Folklore*, LXXI
(1958), 312ff.

known what changes, if any, would occur in the transfer from a free to a fixed form of transmission.

Unfortunately, it cannot be assumed in all cases that the person taking down a poem from dictation has refrained from making changes of his own in the text.[14] For example, the scholar who transcribed some of the songs of M. Krukova, the Russian oral poetess, took it upon himself to "improve" her songs by changing the order of events, removing repetitions, and cutting out some lengthy descriptions.[15] In other words, he revised an acceptable oral text in accordance with what was expected of a literary work. This sort of revision assumes that the scribe would be looking at the work from a literary point of view and removing some of the oral characteristics which would appear redundant or unnecessary in a literary work. In the case of Krukova, it is certain that her scribe had a knowledge of prevailing literary standards and a sense of what was expected in a good literary work.

In turning to the third and final area to be discussed, a matter must now be faced about which there is considerable difference of opinion: the possibility of a text in which there is a mixture of oral and literary style. The problem may be illustrated by referring to the comments of Bowra on Homer. He maintains that the texts of the Homeric poems present us with a paradox, when considered from the point of view of their origin.[16] On the one hand, there is evidence that extensive use has been made of a highly developed oral technique; on the other hand, the author's "purely poetical achievement is far richer and more subtle than any other heroic poet's."[17] As a result, Bowra contends that the only possible solution is that the author was an oral poet who could also write. While this poet still composed in the old way, he took time to revise and improve the text as he wrote it. Such a poet was the kind who would be found in a period of transition from an oral tradition to a literary tradition and such a text might be called a "transitional text."

This notion of a literate oral poet receives support from some scholars of Old and Middle English. R. Diamond claims that it is impossible to tell whether an Anglo-Saxon poem containing oral characteristics was dictated by an oral poet or written by a learned

[14] Lord, "Homer's Originality," p. 127; J. van der Ploeg, "Le rôle de la tradition orale dans la transmission du texte de l'Ancien Testament," *Revue Biblique*, LIV (1947), 17.

[15] Y. M. Sokolov, *Russian Folklore*, trans. C. R. Smith (New York: Macmillan, 1950), p. 677.

[16] *Heroic Poetry*, p. 240.

[17] *Ibid.*

poet who was still using traditional formulas.[18] Moreover, R. A. Waldron has discovered what appear to be formulas in Middle English alliterative poetry of the fourteenth century, a period when most poets were literate. He concludes that the poems were "written by poets who were familiar with a body of formulas which probably originated in a tradition of oral composition and for readers who still retained a taste for conventions of oral style."[19]

In opposition to this view, Lord argues that such a "transitional" text created by an oral poet who has used the advantages of writing to enhance and enrich his poem is impossible.[20] All the richness and subtlety of Homer, and also the great length of the poems, can be accounted for by assuming that the poems were dictated to a scribe. It is certain that the oral poet must have had extraordinary ability and been trained in a highly developed tradition of oral formulaic composition. Lord does agree that it is necessary to assume a transitional *period* in a tradition. By this he means a period when the oral tradition was coming to an end and a literary tradition was beginning. Such a transition is, however, so complex that a long time is required for its completion. Consequently, well-developed oral techniques and well-developed literary techniques would in no case be found in one person at the same point in his life. A singer employs either one technique or the other, but never both at the same time. Lord bases these views on the theory that written and oral techniques are mutually exclusive. This belief grew out of his experience in field-work, in which he discovered that texts written by semi-literate oral poets have not been good. Lord contends that, if we have texts that appear "transitional," it is simply because we do not have enough information to tell whether they are written or oral.[21]

It is too early in the investigation of this subject to make a final decision on the extent to which oral and literary techniques can be employed by a poet in the composition of a poem. The matter is not entirely clear. For instance, while insisting that texts must be oral or written, Lord maintains that "much of the outward mechanics

---

[18] "The Diction of the Signed Poems of Cynewulf," *Philological Quarterly*, XXXVIII (1959), pp. 228f.; see also W. A. O'Neil, "Another Look at Oral Poetry in *The Seafarer*," p. 596; R. Creed, "On the Possibility of Criticizing Old English Poetry," *Texas Studies in Literature and Language*, III (1961), 97. A similar argument is found in S. G. Nichols, Jr., *Formulaic Diction and Thematic Composition in the Chanson de Roland* ("University of North Carolina Studies in the Romance Languages and Literatures," no. 36 [Chapel Hill: University of North Carolina Press, 1961]). Nichols says that "it seems more likely that the poem was written down by someone trained in the oral tradition who may have used the relative leisure of a written endeavour to order the elements in a poem" (p. 9, n. 2).

[19] "Oral-Formulaic Technique and Middle English Alliterative Poetry," *Speculum*, XXXII (1957), 800.

[20] For what follows, see *Singer of Tales*, pp. 128f.; "Homer's Originality," pp. 124–34.

[21] *Singer of Tales*, p. 289, n. 9.

of the oral style, as we have seen, persisted in written poetry, and thus the boundary between the two became blurred and remained blurred to all but the initiate."[22] In other words, in some cases only an expert can decide. Now, if oral characteristics persist in written style to the extent that Lord claims, is not such a text containing a mixture of oral and written styles just the kind of text that the Old and Middle English scholars claim is possible? Should we not, then, hold open the possibility that such texts exist until we receive further clarification and information from future field studies? Certain facts advise caution. It is claimed that early texts, although composed on paper, were written to be read aloud and so still preserve an oral style.[23] Then again, there is a Russian oral poet, Peter Ivanovich Ryabinin-Andreyev, who, according to Sokolov, "is literate and writes down his productions himself."[24] The remark is not explained further. It would be helpful to know more.

[22] *Ibid.*, p. 220. See also his comments on *Digenis Akritas*, pp. 207ff.
[23] H. J. Chaytor, "Reading and Writing," *Explorations*, III (1954), 11.
[24] *Russian Folklore*, p. 676.

4

The Biblical Psalms and
Oral Formulaic Composition

THE CASE for oral formulaic language in the psalms rests upon an accumulation of various kinds of evidence which when brought together form a convincing pattern. This is because the biblical psalms offer limited scope for formulaic analysis. There are several different types of poems from different periods in history, and formulaic material is not found everywhere among these different kinds of poems in great quantity. The kind of evidence to be drawn together consists by and large of the devices and characteristics of oral style already mentioned in some detail. All possible formulas and formulaic systems need to be presented together so that the extent and size of the total body of material may be seen. To these must be added whatever other marks of oral formulaic composition can be discerned. It is equally important to see the way in which the formulas and formulaic phrases cluster in certain psalms. The role, if any, of the theme in the biblical psalms is very difficult to assess and so not a great deal can be said on this subject.

The discussion of oral characteristics in the biblical psalms will vary slightly from the usual approach. The normal way of demonstrating oral formulaic style in oral narrative poems has been to select a group of about twenty-five lines, to underline the matter that can be established as formulaic, and to supply the comparative evidence in notes. For the biblical psalms, however, the phrases that conform to the definition of the formula and the formulaic phrase will be listed first and then the way in which these phrases are distributed among the psalms will be shown afterwards.

When the general definition of oral formulaic devices is applied to a specific poetic tradition, further qualifications may be added, and so before moving on to the evidence the way must be prepared by opening up the question of the nature of formulas in Hebrew poetry. The poetic structure and metre of a given tradition determines what the formulas and formulaic phrases will be like in that tradition. For example, some poetry does not have a strict metre, and so the number of syllables found in a line may vary greatly. It has already been pointed out that previous scholars have allowed certain modifications in the formula as long as the metrical value was not altered. These ran from changes in inflectional endings and the addition or omission of small particles in strict metres to changes in gender, number, tense, and mood in freer metres. Thus, one of the first things to consider is Hebrew poetic structure.

Since the length of formulas and formulaic phrases corresponds to the formal divisions of the poetry in question, we would expect to find formulas occurring in Hebrew to be generally either a line or half-line long since these are the two obvious units of Hebrew poetry. Scholars usually agree on the division of Hebrew poetry into lines. It is also relatively easy to establish where the caesura comes which divides the line into two sections. The various possible relationships between the two parts of the line, usually described by the one term "parallelism," generally make the division within the line obvious. Such a division formed by the caesura is often called a "colon." This term is preferable to "half-line" because it does not imply that every line is divided exactly in half. Furthermore, the term "colon" does not preclude the fact that a line might occasionally have a threefold division. Thus it can be said that the line and the colon, of which the line generally has two, are the most common formal divisions of Hebrew poetry to which possible formulas and formulaic phrases would conform. It should be noted here that there may be times when divisions appear within a colon. This possibility has arisen from the structure of some of the phrases in the list in the next chapter and will be discussed when it appears in the evidence.[1]

While there is general agreement on the division into line and colon, there is no unanimity on what metrical principles, if any, apply within these divisions.[2] Nevertheless, one thing is clear: whatever the metre employed, the number of syllables is variable. It appears that lines and cola could vary considerably in length without disrupting the poetic structure. Thus the general practice will be followed of allowing certain modifications in formulas as long as the change does not disturb the poetic structure.

[1] For a detailed discussion, see the comments to group 20 in the list of phrases in the next chapter.

[2] For a survey of the theories that have been proposed, see the standard introductions to the Old Testament; e.g. O. Eissfeldt, *Einleitung in das Alte Testament* (3rd ed. rev.; Tübingen: J. C. B. Mohr, 1964), pp. 75ff.; see also, S. Mowinckel, *The Psalms in Israel's Worship*, trans. D. R. Ap-Thomas (2 vols.; Oxford: Blackwell, 1962), II, 261–66.

Since an increase or decrease in the number of syllables in a line would not necessarily destroy the poetic structure, and thus render the formulas useless as an aid in composition, quite a number of variations are possible. The addition or omission of the definite article and other elements such as the final pronominal suffixes and the (-ā) ending on the imperative and the first person of the imperfect would certainly be permissible changes. Furthermore, changes of aspect, person, gender, and number should also be allowed in formulas. Although these changes are all types of substitution within a framework, the term "formulaic phrase" will only be applied to phrases in which substitution in some major lexical item occurs.

The latitude permitted in the number of syllables in a colon opens up the possibility of another kind of variation. A formula or formulaic phrase might be expanded by the addition of an extra word which does not belong to the pattern of the formula or formulaic system in question. To add an extra word or structure could not be considered a difficult feat for an oral poet. Furthermore, if all cola do not have the same metrical value, then shorter cola having one metrical value might be changed into longer cola having another metrical value by the addition of a word or structure.[3]

As far as substitution is concerned, one phenomenon that will be noticed among Hebrew formulaic phrases should be mentioned. Usually, since phrases in a formulaic system share a common syntactical pattern, the substitution in one position of the pattern would involve words of the same class. Thus a normal substitution occurs when, for example, a noun is substituted for a noun, a verb for a verb, or a preposition for a preposition. But in twenty-nine groups of the phrases in the next chapter, substitution involves words of different classes.[4] The number of times this occurs provides the justification for recognizing this sort of substitution as a valid possibility. The explanation for this phenomenon may lie in the freedom in the number of syllables in the line. The poets may have been able to substitute quite easily various elements in order to complete a line. The examples show that this sort of free substitution occurs most often at the end of the line although it also occurs frequently at the beginning. Since the evidence is fragmentary, perhaps no satisfactory explanation can be given at this stage. It could be that these phrases in which free substitution occurs may be formulas in their own right which have developed from a common source. This phenomenon will be referred to as "free substitution."

[3] For example, in one commonly used description of Hebrew metre, different lengths are indicated by saying that a colon may have two, three, or four feet. See Eissfeldt, *Einleitung* . . ., p. 84.
[4] See the following groups: 1, 5, 7, 8, 15, 16, 17, 20, 23, 26, 30, 32, 38, 40, 49, 50, 51, 53, 58, 62, 66, 83, 100, 101, 109, 112, 140, 147, and 174.

A small group of examples of free substitution requires further comment. It will be seen that in a number of cases the position in which free substitution takes place occupies about half a colon, the remaining half of the colon being constant.[5] It might be objected that here the constant element or pattern does not fit a formal division of the poetry, in this case the colon, and so such a group of phrases ought not to be called a formulaic system. A closer look at the phrases concerned, however, holds out the possibility of another interpretation. In some cases, the position in which free substitution occurs contains a phrase that is found repeated in other contexts. In other words, it could be considered a short formula. Thus, there are instances in which a colon is composed of two short formulas, each being half a colon long. These could only be called formulas, of course, if it were established that short units half a colon long were natural breaks in the line, which might be called formal divisions in the poetry. The evidence does suggest that a colon could have been broken into two units in Hebrew and that small formulas conforming to this length could have been added together to build a line. But this is not entirely clear since the examples are not extensive. Consequently, this phenomenon will simply be treated as free substitution and further comments will be made in the notes to the evidence.

[5] See examples 17, 20, 23, 30, 37, 38, 58, 109, and 147.

5

Formulas and Formulaic Systems

THIS CHAPTER will cover much the same ground as Chapter 2 and will treat the subject matter in roughly the same order, except that the discussion of theme will find only brief mention at the end of the chapter since little can be said about its role in the composition of psalms. The Hebrew phrases that conform to the definition of the formula and the formulaic phrase have been brought together into appropriate groups. Each group has been given a number for identification and the phrases within each group have been labelled as formulas or formulaic systems. The phrases are normally identified simply by the verse and psalm in which they appear.

The numbered groups have been divided into two classes. Groups 1 to 72 contain three or more phrases which are formulas or belong to formulaic systems. Groups 73 to 175 contain only two such phrases. It would seem better in the interests of sound method to keep phrases occurring three times or more separate from phrases occurring only twice since a single repetition of a phrase is not very strong evidence for its being a formula. Nevertheless, the great number of double occurrences suggests that they form part of the same phenomenon as the phrases that occur three times or more. It is well to recall that the establishment of formulas and formulaic phrases depends upon the amount of material available for comparison. If a great many more psalms had been preserved from Old Testament times, it is possible that many more occurrences of phrases in the following list could be recorded.

In summary, a formula will be a repeated phrase a line or a colon long. The modifications already discussed will be permitted: the addition or omission of the definite article, elements such as the final pronominal suffixes, and the (-ā) ending of the imperative and first person of the imperfect. A formulaic system will include only phrases that have the same essential syntactic structure and at least one major lexical item in common. Again the insistence upon some lexical similarity is only introduced to provide some specific indication that the phrases really do belong together. Any modifications permissible in the formula are also permissible in the pattern of a formulaic system. Formulaic phrases, like formulas, should be a line or colon long. The phenomenon of free substitution discussed above will be allowed in formulaic systems.

The precise manner in which particular groups of phrases conform to the definition of a formula or formulaic phrase is shown in two ways. A system of underlining indicates the words comprising the pattern and identifies the common lexical items. In addition to this, the pattern underlying each formula or system is set down separately in a special abbreviated form. A glance ahead at the list will serve to illustrate the points to be taken up in the following paragraphs.

The underlining may appear as a solid line, a series of dashes, or a series of dots.[1] A solid line is placed under all the morphemes that are lexical constants in a group of phrases. The positions in phrases where normal substitution occurs (that is, where different lexical items from the same word classes are substituted) are underlined with a series of dashes. A series of dots is placed under positions in phrases where free substitution occurs (that is, where different word classes and different structures are substituted). Thus a formula will be underlined completely with a solid line. A formulaic phrase will have a solid line under the lexical constants but a series of dashes under positions where normal substitution occurs. If free substitution is found in a system, then this would be underlined with a series of dots.

Morphemes that appear in some but not all of the phrases in a system or formula cannot be said to belong to the pattern, and so they are not underlined. These are the "additions" or "expansions" spoken of previously. In order to make perfectly clear that words are additions and do not belong to the pattern, they will be enclosed in brackets.

The pattern of each formula or formulaic system will also be clearly emphasized by being set down at the head of the group to which it refers in abbreviations and certain arbitrarily selected signs. The abbreviations are simply shortened forms of the names of the classes of words found in Hebrew. This pattern will be underlined to show the lexical constants and the positions in which substitution occurs. It might seem superfluous to provide such patterns for formulas since formulas are themselves patterns that can change only in small ways. Nevertheless, formulas will be provided with patterns expressed in abbreviations and signs because it will often be necessary to

---

[1] The following system is based on one in common use by scholars investigating formulaic style.

compare the patterns of formulas with those of formulaic systems. Similarities and differences will then be more apparent and more easily described.

The following list contains the abbreviations and arbitrary signs used to present the patterns of formulas and systems. Four classes of Hebrew words have been assumed: nominals, verbals, verbal nouns, and particles.[2] Each of these four main word classes and most of the subclasses have abbreviations. It is not always necessary to indicate the particular subclass to which words belong, since the aim is to present the patterns significantly rather than to present a complete descriptive analysis. There are only three arbitrary signs. Two of these indicate relationships between morphemes; the other stands for a particular type of substitution.

ABBREVIATIONS FOR WORD CLASSES

1. N   a nominal, i.e., a noun or any structure that can take the place of a noun in a syntactical structure.

   n   noun.
   adj   adjective.
   ptc   participle.
   pr   pronoun.
   rel   relative pronoun.
   s   final suffix.
   DN   divine name, standing for "Yahweh," "Elohim," "El," "Adonai," or any of the other proper nouns referring to Yahweh. Final suffixes often attached to many of these words are not indicated. It is generally recognized that the original "Yahweh" has been replaced in most cases by "Elohim" in the Elohist Psalter, Pss. 42–83.[3] Although these words are not strictly speaking lexical constants, the change from one to the other as well as the addition or omission of suffixes could not be viewed as difficult variations for an oral poet to make. Consequently, it is simpler to place all these names with or without suffixes under the one abbreviation.

2. V   a verbal, i.e. a verb or any structure that can substitute for a verb in a syntactical structure.

   v   verb. On a number of occasions a verb will be identified simply as "perf" for perfect, "impf" for imperfect, or "impv" for

[2] The verbal noun or infinitive has been placed in a separate class by E. J. Revell, "A Structural Analysis of the Grammar of the 'Manual of Discipline' (1QS)" (an unpublished thesis for the degree of Doctor of Philosophy at the University of Toronto, 1962). Some of the material from this work has appeared in an article, "The Order of the Elements in the Verbal Statement Clause in 1Q Serek," *Revue de Qumran*, III (1962), 559–69.

[3] S. Mowinckel, *The Psalms in Israel's Worship*, trans. D. R. Ap-Thomas (2 vols.; Oxford: Blackwell, 1962), II, 194. But see the view of R. G. Boling, "'Synonymous' Parallelism in the Psalms," *Journal of Semitic Studies*, V (1960), 221–55.

imperative. The person, gender, and number may also be given, e.g., "3 m sg" for third masculine singular.

3. vn   verbal noun (the so-called infinitive construct). A verbal noun has some of the functions of a noun and some of the functions of a verb. Consequently, in the descriptions of the patterns, it can be considered a nominal when it stands where a noun can stand and it can be considered a verbal when it takes verbal modifiers.

4. Part   particle, i.e., words that do not fit into the classes of nominals, verbals, or verbal nouns.
   p   preposition.
   c   conjunction.
   adv   adverb. This classification includes all such particles as time words, place words, clause modifiers, and verbal modifiers not separately identified. Further analysis is unnecessary for the purposes of this study.
   neg   negative.
   inter interrogative.

ARBITRARY SIGNS

−   joins morphemes within the limits of the word, such as inseparable prepositions, final suffixes, and the conjunction *waw*.

+   stands between two elements, the first of which is bound to the second to make a "bound structure," a term recently suggested as more adequate than the traditional "construct relationship."[4]

x   marks a position in a pattern in which there is a free substitution, i.e., where different word classes or constructions have been substituted.

1

Formula: impv   p – s   n – s

הטה אלי אזנך	Ps. 31:3	*a*
הטה אלי אזנך	Ps. 71:2	*b*
הטה אלי אזנך	Ps. 102:3	*c*

Related system: impv   n – s   p – N

הטה אזנך לרנתי	Ps. 88:3	*d*
הט אזנך לי_(שמע אמרתי)	Ps. 17:6	*e*

[4] J. W. Wevers, "Semitic Bound Structures," *Canadian Journal of Linguistics*, VII (1961), 9–13.

Also in perf: <u>perf   n – s   p – N</u>

(כי) <u>הטה אזנו לי</u>   Ps. 116:1   *f*

Cf. also: <u>impv   n – s   .....x...</u>

<u>הטה</u> (יהוה) <u>אזנך עני</u>.....   Ps. 86:1   *g*

The phrases *a*, *b*, and *c* are a formula and the other phrases appear to be variations of it. The system of *d* and *e* is related to the formula in that it has the same imperative and noun with suffix. Phrase *e* is expanded into a longer colon by the addition of two words, which are found in turn in a system in **4**. Phrase *f* could well be taken as a variation of the system in the perfect aspect. Note also the different suffix on the noun and the added particle. Example *g* could also be taken as a variation of the system with the addition of a DN and a free substitution in the last position of a verb with a suffix instead of a preposition with a nominal.

2

Formula: <u>DN   impv   n – s</u>

<u>אלהים שמע תפלתי</u>   Ps. 54:4   *a*

<u>יהוה שמע תפלתי</u>   Ps. 143:1   *b*

<u>יהוה שמעה תפלתי</u>   Ps. 102:2   *c*

<u>יהוה (אלהים צבאות) שמעה תפלתי</u>   Ps. 84:9   *d*

Variation: <u>impv   n – s   DN</u>

<u>שמעה תפלתי יהוה</u>   Ps. 39:13   *e*

Note the expansion of *d* by the addition of two words. This illustrates how a formula may be expanded to form a longer colon. The change in *e* is one of order only. The DN appears in the final position instead of the initial position. Note also that in *c*, *d*, and *e*, the imperatives have the ending /-ā/. The presence or absence of this ending is one of the variations that was stated earlier to be insignificant for formulaic analysis.

3

System: impv ___ DN ___ n – s

הַאֲזִינָה אֱלֹהִים תְּפִלָּתִי	Ps. 55:2	*a*
הַאֲזִינָה יהוה תְּפִלָּתִי	Ps. 86:6	*b*
שִׁמְעָה אֱלֹהִים רִנָּתִי	Ps. 61:2	*c*

Also in perf: ___ perf ___ DN ___ n – s

שָׁמַע יהוה תְּחִנָּתִי	Ps. 6:10	*d*

Note that *a* and *b* are a formula.

4

System: impv ___ n – s

(שִׁמְעָה יהוה צֶדֶק) הַקְשִׁיבָה רִנָּתִי	Ps. 17:1a	*a*
הַאֲזִינָה תְּפִלָּתִי (בְּלֹא שִׂפְתֵי מִרְמָה)	Ps. 17:1b	*b*
(הַט אָזְנְךָ לִי) שְׁמַע אִמְרָתִי	Ps. 17:6	*c*
הַקְשִׁיבָה תְּפִלָּתִי	Ps. 61:2	*d*

This system can be considered an adaptation of **2** and **3** by the omission of DN. These phrases have no major lexical item in common. However, if **4** is taken with **2** and **3**, each lexical item of **4** occurs at least once more in **2** and **3**, with the sole exception of the noun with the suffix in *c* of **4**. Note that *a*, *b*, and *c* are only parts of cola, if the division of Ps. 17:1 is correct.

5

System: impv ___ n – s ___ x ....

שְׁמַע (יהוה) קוֹלִי אֶקְרָא	Ps. 27:7	*a*
שְׁמַע (אֱלֹהִים) קוֹלִי בְשִׂיחִי	Ps. 64:2	*b*
הַאֲזִינָה קוֹלִי בְּקָרְאִי לָךְ	Ps. 141:1	*c*

The first part of each of these phrases falls into the pattern "impv n – s" and examples *a* and *b* have an added DN. But each phrase is completed with a different kind of element: *a* has an imperfect, *b* has a construction that could be either a preposition with a noun and suffix or a preposition with a verbal noun and suffix, and *c* has a preposition with a verbal noun and suffix and a further preposition and suffix. In other words, the colon is completed with a different construction in each case. This is an example of free substitution.

6

System: _impv   n + n – s_

(וְ)הַקֲשִׁיבָה (בְּ)קוֹל תַּחֲנוּנוֹתַי	Ps. 86:6	*a*
הַאֲזִינָה (יהוה) קוֹל תַּחֲנוּנַי	Ps. 140:7	*b*
שְׁמַע קוֹל תַּחֲנוּנַי	Ps. 28:2a	*c*

Also in perf: _perf   n + n – s_

הִקְשִׁיב (בְּ)קוֹל תְּפִלָּתִי	Ps. 66:19	*d*
(אָכֵן) שָׁמַעְתָּ קוֹל תַּחֲנוּנַי	Ps. 31:23bα	*e*

Another variation in perf: part   perf   n + n – s

כִּי שָׁמַע (יהוה) קוֹל בִּכְיִי	Ps. 6:9	*f*
כִּי שָׁמַע קוֹל תַּחֲנוּנַי	Ps. 28:6	*g*

c and *f* as full-line formula: v   n + n – s   p – vn – s   p – s

שְׁמַע קוֹל תַּחֲנוּנַי בְּשַׁוְּעִי אֵלֶיךָ	Ps. 28:2	*h*
(אָכֵן) שָׁמַעְתָּ קוֹל תַּחֲנוּנַי בְּשַׁוְּעִי אֵלֶיךָ	Ps. 31:23b	*i*

Phrase added to *c* and *f* is a formula: p – vn – s   p – s

בְּשַׁוְּעִי אֵלֶיךָ	Ps. 28:2b	*j*
בְּשַׁוְּעִי אֵלֶיךָ	Ps. 31:23bβ	*k*

The system of *f* and *g* could be a variation of either *a*, *b*, and *c* or *d* and *e*. Phrase *g* may not be a colon.

7

System: n – s   p   DN ___ impf 1 sg___

קוֹלִי אֶל יהוה אֶקְרָא	Ps. 3:5	*a*
קוֹלִי אֶל יהוה אֶזְעַק	Ps. 142:2a	*b*
קוֹלִי אֶל יהוה אֶתְחַנָּן	Ps. 142:2b	*c*

Related system: n – s   p   DN   x_{.....}

קוֹלִי אֶל אלהים וָאֶצְעָקָה	Ps. 77:2a	*d*
קוֹלִי אֶל אלהים וְהַאֲזִין אֵלָי	Ps. 77:2b	*e*

The system of *d* and *e* begins with exactly the same words as the
system of *a*, *b*, and *c* but the two phrases are completed differently:
d with conjunction and imperfect and *e* with conjunction and
imperative plus a preposition with a suffix. For this reason these
have been called a free substitution, although, it should be noted,
both are verbal constructions and to this extent do not depart radically
from the pattern of the system of *a*, *b*, and *d*.

8

Formula: p – s   DN   impf 1 sg___

אֵלֶיךָ יהוה אֶקְרָא	Ps. 30:9	*a*
אֵלֶיךָ יהוה אֶקְרָא	Joel 1:19	*b*
אֵלֶיךָ יהוה אֶקְרָא (צוּרִי)	Ps. 28:1	*c*

Related system: x_{.....}   p – s   impf 1 sg___

מִקְצֵה הָאָרֶץ אֵלֶיךָ אֶקְרָא	Ps. 61:3	*d*
(כִּי) אֵלֶיךָ אֶקְרָא כָל הַיּוֹם	Ps. 86:3	*e*

Note that the free substitution precedes in *d* but follows in *e*.
This system can be taken as a variation of the preceding formula
because the preposition with suffix and the verb is the same in all
phrases. Examples *d* and *e* also provide a good illustration of free
substitution. The x element in *d* is a prepositional phrase but in *e*
it is not. They both function, however, as verbal modifiers. Phrase *e*
may not be a colon.

4

Cf. also: <u>perf 1 sg   p – s   DN</u>

זָעַקְתִּי אֵלֶיךָ יְהוָה   Ps. 142:6   *f*

יְהוָה (אֱלֹהַי) שִׁוַּעְתִּי אֵלֶיךָ (וַתִּרְפָּאֵנִי)   Ps. 30:3   *g*

In *g* DN precedes and the phrase has been expanded to a full line.

<u>p – s</u>   <u>DN   perf 1 sg</u>

(וַאֲנִי) אֵלֶיךָ יְהוָה שִׁוַּעְתִּי   Ps. 88:14   *h*

The last three phrases, *f*, *g*, and *h*, can only be considered as possible variations of the preceding formula and system. The change in word order creates the difficulty: the DN is in a different position in each and the preposition with suffix follows the verb in *f* and *g* but precedes in *h*. There are not enough examples of changes in word order in formulas and formulaic phrases to be able to judge whether such examples should be accepted or rejected as legitimate variants.

9

Formula: <u>p – s   DN   n – s   impf 1 sg</u>

אֵלֶיךָ יְהוָה נַפְשִׁי אֶשָּׂא   Ps. 25:1   *a*

(כִּי) אֵלֶיךָ אֲדֹנָי נַפְשִׁי אֶשָּׂא   Ps. 86:4   *b*

Variation in the perf: <u>p – s   perf 1 sg   n – s</u>

(כִּי) אֵלֶיךָ נָשָׂאתִי נַפְשִׁי   Ps. 143:8   *c*

אֵלֶיךָ נָשָׂאתִי (אֶת) עֵינַי   Ps. 123:1   *d*

The system of *c* and *d* has been considered a variant of the preceding formula because of the common lexical items.

10

System: <u>v   p – s   N</u>

תָּבוֹא לְפָנֶיךָ תְּפִלָּתִי   Ps. 88:3   *a*

(וַ)תָּבוֹא אֵלֶיךָ תְּפִלָּתִי   Jon. 2:8   *b*

תָּבוֹא לְפָנֶיךָ אֶנְקַת אָסִיר   Ps. 79:11   *c*

Note that the final noun and its suffix are lexical constants in *a* and *b*.

Related system: c – n – s   p – s   v

ושועתי אליך תבוא   Ps. 102:2   *d*

ושועתי לפניו תבוא (באזניו)   Ps. 18:7   *e*

The system of *d* and *e* has the same forms as the system of *a* and *b* but they are in a different order. The verb is the same throughout. The suffix is different in *e* but this is one of changes permitted to a formula.

Cf. also: v · n – s   p – s

תבוא תחנתי לפניך   Ps. 119:170   *f*

This last phrase has the same forms as the others, the verb being a lexical constant, but the order is different from that of either of the preceding systems.

11

Formula: impv   p – s   c – impv – s

פנה אלי וחנני   Ps. 25:16   *a*

פנה אלי וחנני   Ps. 86:16   *b*

פנה אלי וחנני   Ps. 119:132   *c*

12

System: impv – s   p – n – s

הושיעני בחסדך   Ps. 31:17   *a*

הושיעני כחסדך   Ps. 109:26   *b*

הושיעני למען חסדך   Ps. 6:5   *c*

Note that in *c* a separable preposition is substituted for the inseparable preposition of *a* and *b*.

13

System: <u>impv – s</u>   <u>DN</u>   <u>N – s</u>

הורני יהוה דַרכֶךָ   Ps. 27:11   *a*

הורני יהוה דַרכֶךָ (אהלך באמתך)   Ps. 86:11   *b*

הורני יהוה דֶרֶך חֻקֶיךָ   Ps. 119:33   *c*

Phrase *b* has been expanded to a longer colon by the addition of two words. These words appear as a formula in group **106**.

14

System: <u>impv – s</u>   <u>p – N – s</u>

הצילני מרֹדפי   Ps. 142:7a   *a*

הצילני מאיֹבי (יהוה)   Ps. 143:9   *b*

הצילני מאיֹבי (אלהי)   Ps. 59:2   *c*

(בידך עתתי) הצילני מיד אויֹבי (ומדרפי)   Ps. 31:16   *d*

Note that *d* is an expansion to a full line.

Also in impf: <u>impf – s</u>   <u>p – n – s</u>

יצילני מאיֹבי (עז)   Ps. 18:18a   *e*

a and *e* as a full-line system:

<u>v – s</u>   <u>p – N – s</u>   <u>part   v   p – s</u>

הצילני מרֹדפי כי אמצו ממני   Ps. 142:7   *f*

יצילני מאיֹבי (עז ומשנאי) כי אמצו ממני   Ps. 18:18   *g*

Phrase added to *a* and *e* is a formula: <u>part   v   p – s</u>

כי אמצו ממני   Ps. 142:7b   *h*

(ומשנאי) כי אמצו ממני   Ps. 18:18b   *i*

15

System: <u>impv   n – s   x</u>
                                   .....

Ps. 9:14   *a*   (חנני יהוה) <u>ראה עניי</u> משנאי

Ps. 25:18   *b*   <u>ראה עניי</u> ועמלי

Ps. 119:153   *c*   <u>ראה עניי</u> וחלצני

Phrase *a* has an addition of two words which appear as constant
in **16**. This is another example of a free substitution. The last element
in each phrase is different: in *a*, a preposition followed by a participle
with a suffix; in *b*, a conjunction followed by a noun with a suffix;
and in *c*, a conjunction followed by an imperative with a suffix. In
other words the colon has been completed in each with a different
construction.

16

System: <u>impv – s   DN   part   x</u>
                                                  .....

Ps. 6:3 a   *a*   <u>חנני יהוה</u> כי אמלל אני

Ps. 31:10   *b*   <u>חנני יהוה</u> כי צר לי

Ps. 56: 2   *c*   <u>חנני אלהים</u> כי שאפני אנוש

Ps. 86:3   *d*   <u>חנני אדני</u> כי אליך אקרא כל היום

Related system: <u>impv – s   DN   part   x</u>
                                                         .....

Ps. 6:3b   *e*   <u>רפאני יהוה</u> כי נבהלו עצמי

Ps. 26:1   *f*   <u>שפטני יהוה</u> כי אני בתמי הלכתי

Ps. 69:17   *g*   <u>ענני יהוה</u> כי טוב חסדך

Phrase *d* is a full line. The x element is in each case a clause
introduced by a particle which is part of the pattern. The structure
and lexical content of each clause is different, although they each
present a motivation for the prayer expressed in the imperative. The
x element of *d* appears also in **8**. For *g*, see also **38**.

17

System: <u>impv</u> <u>n – s</u>   <u>x</u>

שמרה נפשי והצילני	Ps. 25:20	a
שמרה נפשי כי חסיד אני	Ps. 86:2	b
פלטה נפשי מרשע חרבך	Ps. 17:13	c
(יהוה) הצילה נפשי משפת שקר	Ps. 120:2	d

Also: x   <u>impv</u> <u>n – s</u>

שובה יהוה חלצה נפשי	Ps. 6:5	e
אנה יהוה מלטה נפשי	Ps. 116:4	f

The basic pattern of an imperative followed by a noun with a suffix may serve as a colon itself without any additions as in **4**. Often such a short phrase can be expanded by a DN as in **2** and **3** or another noun as in **6**. In this case, however, the extra element varies from a conjunction followed by an imperative with suffix in *a* to a clause in *b*. Note that the x element precedes in *e* and *f*.

18

System: <u>p – n – s</u>   <u>impv – s</u>

בצדקתך פלטני	Ps. 31:2	a
בצדקתך חיני	Ps. 119:40	b

Variant in impf: <u>p – n – s</u>   <u>impf – s</u>

בצדקתך תצילני (ותפלטני)	Ps. 71:2	c

Possibly related: <u>p – n – s</u>   <u>impv – s</u>

באמנתך עני (בצדקתך)	Ps. 143:1	d
(אלהים) בשמך הושיעני	Ps. 54:3	e

While phrases *d* and *e* have the same pattern as the system of *a* and *b*, there are no constant, major lexical items linking these two phrases with the system. On the other hand, the fact that the preposition and suffixes are the same suggests that *d* and *e* may be variants of the system created by substituting in both noun and verb positions. Furthermore, it should be noted that the added construction in *d* is the constant in *a*, *b*, and *c*.

19

System: <u>DN</u>   p – n – s   impv

יהוה <u>לעזרתי חושה</u>   Ps 40:14   *a*

אלהי <u>לעזרתי חישה</u>   Ps. 17:12   *b*

אילותי <u>לעזרתי חושה</u>   Ps. 22:20   *c*

Cf. also: impv   p – n – s   <u>DN</u>

<u>חושה לעזרתי אדני</u> (תשועתי)   Ps. 38:23   *d*

Phrase *d*, which has been expanded to a full line, has the same
lexical items as the others but in a different order. It is possible that
it is a variation of the system.

20

System: x   impv   impv – s

כי צר לי <u>מהר עני</u>   Ps. 69:18   *a*

ביום אקרא <u>מהר עני</u>   Ps. 102:3   *b*

Also: impv   impv – s   x

<u>מהר עני</u> יהוה   Ps. 143:7   *c*

In examples *a* and *b* the constant part of the phrases amounts to
about half a colon. This is one of the systems suggesting that formal
divisions smaller than the colon are occasionally apparent so that a
colon may be viewed as being composed of two units about half a
colon long. Thus formulas and formulaic phrases corresponding to
these small units could be added together to form a colon. For
example, the x element in phrase *a* is found in **30** as the constant
part of the pattern. One could say, then, that phrase *a* is a colon
composed of two small formulas. Furthermore, the x element in
20, 30, and some others does not have a fixed position but sometimes
precedes and sometimes follows the constant element. This also
suggests that we are dealing with two units within the colon. For
other examples of this kind of x element, see **17, 23, 30, 37, 38, 58,
109**, and **147**. All the phrases included in these groups do not divide
into two units, e.g., phrase **20c**, and so for this and other reasons
already mentioned these groups have been regularly treated as a
system of colon length with free substitution.

21

Formula: neg   v   n − s   p − s

אל תסתר פניך ממני Ps. 27:9 *a*

אל תסתר פניך ממני Ps. 102:3 *b*

אל תסתר פניך ממני Ps. 143:7 *c*

Variation: neg   v   n − s   p − N

(ו)אל תסתר פניך מעבדך Ps. 69:18 *d*

Also as inter: inter   v   n − s   p − s

עד אנה תסתיר (את) פניך ממני Ps. 13:2 *e*

למה (יהוה תזנח נפשי) תסתיר פניך ממני Ps. 88:15 *f*

Also in perf: neg   v   n − s   p − s

(ו)לא הסתיר פניו ממנו Ps. 22:25 *g*

This group of phrases illustrates many of the variations that occur. By substitution in different positions, a formula may be adapted to various uses. Phrase *d* substitutes a noun with a suffix for an original suffix. Phrases *e* and *f* are interrogatives rather than negatives. Note how *f* has been expanded to a full line by the addition of three words following the interrogative. Phrase *g* is a negative statement in the perfect aspect rather than the negative of the imperative. Observe also the change of person in the suffixes.

22

Formulas: DN   neg   v   p − s

אדני אל תרחק ממני Ps. 35:22 *a*

אלהי אל תרחק ממני Ps. 38:22 *b*

אלהים אל תרחק ממני Ps. 71:12 *c*

Also in a shorter form: neg   v   p − s

אל תרחק ממני Ps. 22:12 *d*

Variation: ___neg__ _v_ _ _n – s_ _____

Ps. 28:1   אל תחרש ממני   *e*

Possible variation: ___DN___ ___neg___ _v_

Ps. 22:20   (ואתה) יהוה אל תרחק   *f*

It was stated earlier that most forms of DN with or without suffixes
were to be considered constants. Both *d* and *e* are shorter forms of
the formula, DN being omitted. In *e* there is substitution in the verb.
Phrase *f* could be considered a variation of the formula in which
the preposition has been dropped and a conjunction followed by a
pronoun placed at the beginning. Phrase *d* may or may not be a full
colon.

23

System: .....x.... ___neg___ _v_ _____

Ps. 35:22   ראיתה יהוה אל תחרש   *a*

Ps. 39:13   אל דמעתי אל תחרש   *b*

Ps. 109:1   אלהי תהלתי אל תחרש   *c*

Cf. also: ___neg___ _v_ .....x....

Ps. 83:1   אל תחרש ואל תשקט אל   *d*

Phrase *e* of **22** could have been listed here with *d*. The constant
here looks as though it could be a small formula useful in building
cola. See the comments to **20**. The division of Ps. 39:13 into cola is
not clear.

24

System: _v_ _ _p_ _ _n + n_ _____

Ps. 28:1   (ו)נמשלתי עם יורדי בור   *a*

Ps. 143:7   (ו)נמשלתי עם ירדי בור   *b*

Ps. 88:5   נחשבתי עם יורדי בור   *c*

25

System: ____v____n____n____p – s____

טמנו גאים פח לי   Ps. 140:6   *a*

נתנו רשעים פח לי   Ps. 119:110   *b*

טמנו פח לי   Ps. 142:4   *c*

Phrase *c* omits the first noun.

26

System: ____perf 3 pl____ptc – s____x....

(ו)רבו שנאי שקר   Ps. 38:20   *a*

רבו (משערות ראשי) שנאי חנם   Ps. 69:5   *b*

Although to label the last elements of these phrases as x is strictly correct since the word in *a* is of the noun class and the word in *b* is of the particle class, both words perform the same syntactic function. Note the expansion in *b*.

Cf. also: ____perf 3 pl____ptc – s____x....

עצמו (מצמיתי) איבי שקר   Ps. 69:5   *c*

Phrase *c* has the same pattern as the above system but no lexical items in common except the suffix, although the x element in *c* is the same as that in *a*.

Phrase *b* forms another system: ____perf 3 pl____p – n + n – s____

רבו משערות ראשי (שנאי חנם)   Ps. 69:5   *b*

עצמו משערות ראשי   Ps. 40:13   *d*

Note the combinations:

ואיבי חיים עצמו ורבו שנאי שקר   Ps. 38:20   *a*

רבו (משערות ראשי) שנאי חנם   Ps. 69:5   *b*

עצמו (מצמיתי) איבי שקר   *c*

The first colon of Ps. 38:20 has not been listed above but it should be noted that it has the same verb as *c* and the same noun with suffix as *c*. Is the plural noun a mistake for the x element in *b*?

27

Formula: <u>perf 3 pl – s   n + n</u>

אפפוני חבלי מות   Ps. 18:5   *a*

אפפוני חבלי מות   Ps. 116:3   *b*

Also: <u>perf 3 pl – s   n + n</u>

קדמוני מוקשי מות   Ps. 18:6   *c*

Phrase *c* can be put in a system with *a* and *b* with the last noun as the constant lexical item.

Possible variant system: <u>n + n   perf 3 pl – s</u>

חבלי שאול סבבוני   Ps. 18:6   *d*

(ו)דברי שנאה סבבוני   Ps. 109:3   *e*

Possible variant: <u>n + n   perf 3 pl – s</u>

(ו)מצרי שאול מצאוני   Ps. 116:3   *f*

These two systems have been placed together because they have some features in common. Phrases *a*, *b*, and *c* have the same forms as *d*, *e*, and *f*. The verbs in *a* and *b* and *d* and *e* are double ʿayin verbs and have a similar meaning. The order is different in both systems but one may have developed from the other. Phrase *f* can be considered a possible variant because the second noun is the same as the second noun in *d*.

28

Formula: <u>v   p – s   n – s   n + n – s</u>

פצו עליך פיהם כל אויביך   Lam. 2:16   *a*

פצו עלינו פיהם כל אויבינו   Lam. 3:46   *b*

Both of these are a full line. Note the change in person in the suffixes, an insignificant change in a formula.

The first cola of *a* and *b* make a formula: <u>v   p – s   n – s</u>

פצו עליך פיהם   Lam. 2:16   *c*

פצו עלינו פיהם   Lam. 3:46   *d*

פצו עלי פיהם   Ps. 22:14   *e*

Variant: v p – s n – s

ויֿרחיבו עלי פיהם Ps. 35:21 *f*

Phrase *f* can form a system with *c*, *d*, and *e* with substitution in the verb.

29

System: V p – s n – s

(ב)התעטף עלי רוחי Ps. 142:4 *a*

(ו)תתעטף עלי רוחי Ps. 143:4 *b*

(ב)התעטף עלי נפשי Jon. 2:8 *c*

The verbal noun is considered here as a verbal since it is a verb substitute.

30

System: x part n p – s

חנני יהוה כי צר לי Ps. 31:10 *a*

ראה יהוה כי צר לי Lam. 1:20 *b*

Cf. also: part n p – s x

כי צר לי מהר ענני Ps. 69:18 *c*

For this sort of x element in which the constant part is approximately half the colon, see the comments to **20**. Note in addition that the x element in *a* is a constant in **16**. Thus both the x element in *a* and the x element in *c* are found as constants elsewhere.

31

System: part n c – n pr

כי עני ואביון אני Ps. 86:1 *a*

כי עני ואביון אנכי Ps. 109:22 *b*

כי יחיד ועני אני Ps. 25:16 *c*

Variant system: c – pr   n   c – n

ואני עני ואביון	Ps. 40:18	d
ואני עני וכואב	Ps. 69:30	e

32

System: pr   v   N – s

אתה ידעת חרפתי	Ps. 69:20	a
(ו)אתה ידעת נתיבתי	Ps. 142:4	b
אתה ידעת שבתי (וקומי)	Ps. 139:2	c
אתה ידעת מוצא שפתי	Jer. 17:16	d

In c the nominal is a verbal noun, which can function as a noun substitute. The added element simply repeats the same construction.
Cf. also:

(אלהים) אתה ידעת (ל)אולתי	Ps. 69:6	e

Note that e has the same pattern and lexical constants as the other phrases except that a preposition stands before the noun.

33

Formula: perf 1 sg   DN – s   pr

אמרתי אלהי אתה	Ps. 31:15	a
אמרתי (ליהוה) אלי אתה	Ps. 140:7	b

Variant systems: perf   pr   n – s

אמרתי אתה מחסי	Ps. 142:6	c
אמרת (ליהוה אדני) אתה טובתי	Ps. 16:2	d

In the system the pronoun follows the verb. In d the verb is pointed as a second feminine singular but should likely be pointed as a first person singular. From the point of view of formulaic analysis, however, a change of person is not significant.

34

System: <u>part</u>   <u>pr</u>   <u>N – s</u>

כי אתה מעוזי	Ps. 31:5	*a*
כי אתה תקותי (אדני)	Ps. 71:5	*b*
כי אתה (יהוה) מחסי	Ps. 91:9	*c*
כי אתה אלוהי	Ps. 143:10	*d*
כי אתה אלהי מעוזי	Ps. 43:2	*e*
כי אתה אלהי ישעי	Ps. 25:5	*f*

Possible variant:

כי אתה גחי (מבטן)	Ps. 22:10	*g*

Example *g* might be a variant with a participle as the nominal and an added prepositional phrase.

35

System: <u>n – s</u>   <u>c – n – s</u>   <u>pr</u>

(כי) סלעי ומצודתי אתה	Ps. 71:3	*a*
(כי) סלעי ומצודתי אתה	Ps. 31:4	*b*
עזרתי ומפלטי אתה	Ps. 40:18	*c*
סתרי ומגני אתה	Ps. 119:114	*d*

Note that *a* and *b* are identical and could be considered a formula.

36

System: <u>part</u>   <u>v</u>   <u>n</u>   <u>p – N</u>

כי היית משגב לי	Ps. 59:17	*a*
כי היית מחסה לי	Ps. 61:4	*b*
כי היית עזרתה לי	Ps. 63:8	*c*
כי היית מעוז לדל	Is. 25:4	*d*

Note that in *d* a noun has been substituted after the preposition where a suffix stands in the others.

37

Formula: p – s   DN   v   neg   v   p – n

בך יהוה חסיתי אל אבושה לעולם	Ps. 31:2 *a*
בך יהוה חסיתי אל אבושה לעולם	Ps. 71:1 *b*

Possible variation: p – s   _   v   neg   v

(אלהי) בך בטחתי אל אבושה	Ps. 25:2 *c*

In *c* the DN is questionable since it disturbs the acrostic order in the psalm. Otherwise the phrase is a shortened version of the formula with substitution in the verb.

Cf. also the system: x   part   v   p – s

אל אבוש כי חסיתי בך	Ps. 25:20 *d*
שמרני אל כי חסיתי בך	Ps. 16:1 *e*

Possible variation: part   p – s   v

כי בך בטחתי	Ps. 143:8 *f*

In *f* the order is different and thus it can be considered only a possible variation. The formula of *a* and *b* and the system of *d* and *e* have been treated together because they have certain forms and lexical items in common. There is a possibility that they are variants.

The system of *d* and *e* has free substitution and requires further comment. The constant part of the phrases is a clause, as in **30** and **38**. In all these examples the clause never makes up a colon by itself but is always supplemented by another element. Except in **38a**, this x element is a verbal construction. In three examples, **38b**, **38c**, and **37e**, the verb is an imperative with a suffix. See the comments to **20** and **30**.

38

System: part   adj   n – s   x

כי טוב חסדך מחיים	Ps. 63:4 *a*
כי טוב חסדך הצילני	Ps. 109:21 *b*

Also:

עני יהוה כי טוב חסדך	Ps. 69:17 *c*

Note that the x element precedes in *c* and this phrase is also listed in **16**. See the comments to **37**.

39

Formula: <u>DN inter p – s</u>

יהוה מי כמוך Ps. 35:10	*a*
אלהים מי כמוך Ps. 71:19	*b*
יהוה (אלהי צבאות) מי כמוך Ps. 89:9	*c*

40

System: <u>impf 3 pl c – impf 3 pl N + n – s</u>

יבשו יכלו שטני נפשי Ps. 71:13a	*a*
יבשו ויכלמו מבקשי נפשי Ps. 35:4a	*b*
יבשו ויחפרו (יחד) מבקשי נפשי (לספותה) Ps. 40:15a	*c*
יבשו ויחפרו (יחדו) שמחי רעתי Ps. 35:26a	*d*

Examples *a*, *b*, *c*, and *d* are full lines. Phrase *a* lacks a conjunction. Taken alone, *a* and *b* have a further lexical constant in the noun with the suffix. Taken alone, *c* and *d* have a further lexical constant in the verb with the conjunction. These phrases also have added elements which are two forms of the same adverb.

Cf. also :

יבשו ויבהלו מאד כל איבי ישבו יבשו רגע Ps. 6:11	*e*
יבשו ויבהלו עדי עד ויחפרו ויאבדו Ps. 83:18	*f*

These two phrases are not offered as an example of a system, since the correspondence of lexical items, forms, and structure is only partial. They do contain sufficient similarities, however, to merit attention. The first two words in each are the same. The pattern of these two words is the same as the pattern of the first two words in the preceding system, the first verb being the constant. These two phrases may have originally been variants of the system *a*, *b*, *c*, and *d*.

Cf. also the system:

<u>impf 3 pl n c – impf 3 pl N + n – s</u>

יסגו אחור ויחפרו חשבי רעתי Ps. 35:4b	*g*
יסגו אחור ויכלמו חפצי רעתי Ps. 40:15b	*h*

These are full lines. Except for the noun following the first verb, the pattern is the same as that of the system *a*, *b*, *c*, and *d*, although there are no lexical constants which continue through both systems. There are, however, some lexical similarities. The verb with the conjunction in *g* is the same as the verb with the conjunction in *c* and *d*. The noun with the suffix in *g* and *h* is the same as the noun with the suffix in *d*. Finally the verb with the conjunction in *h* is the same as the verb with the conjunction in *b*.

Cf. also the system: impf 3 pl   n   c – n   x

ילבשו בשת וכלמה המגדילים עלי	Ps. 35:26b	*i*
יעטו חרפה וכלמה מבקשי רעתי	Ps. 71:13b	*j*

Note that the x elements in these phrases are really quite similar: a participle with a prepositional phrase in *i* and a participle bound to a noun with a suffix in *j*.

Cf. also:

(כי) בשו כי חפרו מבקשי רעתי	Ps. 71:24	*k*
יבשו ויסגו אחור כל שנאי ציון	Ps. 129:5	*l*

These phrases do not have a pattern in common but they do have lexical similarities with the phrases already presented. These have been underlined.

Note the following combinations:

יבשו ויכלמו מבקשי נפשי	Ps. 35:4	*b*
יסגו אחור ויחפרו חשבי רעתי		*g*
יבשו ויחפרו (יחדו) שמחי רעתי	Ps. 35:26	*d*
ילבשו בשת וכלמה המגדילים עלי		*i*
יבשו ויחפרו (יחד) מבקשי נפשי (לספותה)	Ps. 40:15	*c*
יסגו אחור ויכלמו חפצי רעתי		*h*
יבשו יכלו שטני נפשי יעטו חרפה וכלמה מבקשי רעתי	Ps. 71:13	

The last line is a combination of *a* and *j*.

All these phrases have been underlined as they were when first presented. Further similarities can be seen when these combinations are examined. For example, in the extracts from Pss. 35:4 and 40:15, the first lines of each, *b* and *c*, are from the same system and the last lines of each, *g* and *h*, come from the same system. Furthermore, the participle with the suffixed noun in the first lines, *a* and *b*, is the same.

41

System: V   N   DN

(ו)אזמרה שם יהוה עליון	Ps. 7:18	*a*
אזמרה שמך עליון	Ps. 9:3	*b*
(ול)זמר (ל)שמך עליון	Ps. 92:2	*c*

The verbal in *c* is a verbal noun, which is a verb substitute. The nominal in *a* is a bound structure with two nouns, while in *b* and *c* it is a noun with a suffix.

42

System: impf 1 sg   n – s   p – N

(כן) אזמרה שמך לעד	Ps. 61:9	*a*
(ו)אכבדה שמך לעולם	Ps. 86:12	*b*
(ו)אברכה שמך לעולם ועד	Ps. 145:1	*c*
(ו)אהללה שמך לעולם ועד	Ps. 145:2	*d*
אספרה שמך לאחי	Ps. 22:23	*e*

Note that all the imperfects have the /-ā/ ending.

43

Formula: part   v   p – s

כי גמל עלי	Ps. 13:6	*a*
כי תגמל עלי	Ps. 142:8	*b*
כי (יהוה) גמל עליכי	Ps. 116:7	*c*

The only variations are a change in the aspect of the verb and a change in the person of the suffix, both of which are being taken as insignificant changes for formulaic analysis.

44

System: _perf 2 m sg_   _n – s_   _p – N_

Ps. 56:14   (כי) הצלת נפשי ממות   *a*

Ps. 116:8   (כי) חלצת נפשי ממות   *b*

Ps. 86:13   (ו)הצלת נפשי משאול תחתיה   *c*

The nominal in *c* is a noun with an adjective. See also **188**.

45

System: c   pr   v   p – n – s

Ps. 30:7   ואני אמרתי בשלוי   *a*

Ps. 31:23   ואני אמרתי בחפזי   *b*

Ps. 116:11   אני אמרתי בחפזי   *c*

Cf. also: c   pr   v   p – N – s

Is. 38:10   ואני אמרתי בדמי ימי   *d*

Note that the conjunction is lacking in *c*. Phrase *d* can be placed in a system with the others.

Cf. also: c   pr   v   _perf 1 sg_   p   n – s

Ps. 31:23   ואני אמרתי (בחפזי) נגרזתי מנגד עיניך   *e*

Jon. 2:5   ואני אמרתי נגרשתי מנגד עיניך   *f*

Phrase *e* is simply *b* as a full line, which forms a system with *f*.

46

System: _neg_   v   p – N

Ps. 15:5   לא ימוט לעולם   *a*

Ps. 30:7   בל אמוט לעולם   *b*

Ps. 10:6   בל אמוט לדר ודר   *c*

Possible variation: p – N   _neg_   v

Ps. 112:6   (כי) לעולם לא ימוט   *d*

In *d* the order is different and so it can only be considered a possible variation. The texts of Ps. 10:6 and Ps. 15:5 both offer some difficulty with respect to the proper division into line and colon. The negative in *a* is lexically different from the negatives in *b* and *c* but the change from one to the other can hardly be considered significant in formulaic analysis.

47

System: p – n + n – s   v

בצל כנפיך תסתירני	Ps. 17:8	*a*
בצל כנפיך יחסיון	Ps. 36:8	*b*
(ו)בצל כנפיך אחסה	Ps. 57:2	*c*
(ו)בצל כנפיך ארנן	Ps. 63:8	*d*

Cf. also: v   p – n + n – s

תסתירם בסתר פניך	Ps. 31:21	*e*
אחסה בסתר כנפיך	Ps. 61:5	*f*

The system *e* and *f* was included here because it has some similarities with the preceding. The verb in *f* is the same as the verb in *c*. The noun with a suffix in *f* is the same as the noun with a suffix in *a*, *b*, *c*, and *d*. The verb in *e* is the same as the verb in *a*. All these suggest that the two systems are related.

48

Formula: impv pl   p – DN   n   adj

שירו ליהוה שיר חדש	Ps. 96:1	*a*
שירו ליהוה שיר חדש	Ps. 98:1	*b*
שירו ליהוה שיר חדש	Ps. 149:1	*c*
שירו ליהוה שיר חדש	Is. 42:10	*d*

Variation: impv pl p – N   n   adj

שירו לו שיר חדש	Ps. 33:3	*e*

See also **49***d*.

49

Formula: impv pl   p – DN   N

הריעו לאלהים כל הארץ	Ps. 66:1	*a*
הריעו ליהוה כל הארץ	Ps. 98:4	*b*
הריעו ליהוה כל הארץ	Ps. 100:1	*c*

Variant: impv pl   p – DN   N

שירו ליהוה כל הארץ	Ps. 96:1	*d*

Cf. also: impv pl   p – DN   x

הריעו לאלהים בקול רנה	Ps. 47:2	*e*

In *d* there is substitution in the verb. In *e* a prepositional phrase is found in the position where the vocative stands in the others.

50

System: impv pl   p – DN   p – n

הודו ליהוה בכנור	Ps. 33:2	*a*
זמרו ליהוה בכנור	Ps. 98:5	*b*
זמרו לאלהינו בכנור	Ps. 147:7	*c*

Related system: impv pl   p – DN   x

זמרו ליהוה ישב ציון	Ps. 9:12	*d*
זמרו ליהוה חסידיו	Ps. 30:5	*e*

The x elements in the last two phrases are both nominals but have different functions, the one in *d* being in apposition and the one in *e* being a vocative. Thus it must be considered a position of free substitution.

51

System: impv pl   p – DN   impv pl   n – s

שירו לאלהים זמרו שמו	Ps. 68:5	*a*
שירו ליהוה ברכו שמו	Ps. 96:2	*b*

Ps. 105:1   הודו ליהוה קראו (ב)שמו   *c*

Is. 12:4   הודו ליהוה קראו (ב)שמו   *d*

Variation: <u>impv pl   p – N   impv pl   n – s</u>

Ps. 100:4   הודו לו ברכו שמו   *e*

Cf. also: <u>impv pl   p – N   impv pl   x</u>

Ps. 105:2   שירו לו זמרו לו   *f*

Phrase *f* may be compared with *a* for common lexical items. It is a possible variation.

52

System: <u>impv pl   p – n   n – s</u>

Ps. 9:12   הגידו בעמים עלילותיו   *a*

Ps. 105:1   הודיעו בעמים עלילותיו   *b*

Is. 12:4   הודיעו בעמים עלילתיו   *c*

Also: <u>impv pl   p – N   n – s</u>

Ps. 96:3   ספרו (בגוים כבודו) ב(כל) העמים נפלאותיו   *d*

Note the expansion to a full line in *d*.

53

Formula: <u>ptc   n   c – n</u>

Ps. 115:15   עשה שמים וארץ   *a*

Ps. 121:2b   עשה שמים וארץ   *b*

Ps. 124:8b   עשה שמים וארץ   *c*

Ps. 134:3   עשה שמים וארץ   *d*

Ps. 146:6   עשה שמים וארץ   *e*

b and *c* as a full-line system:

<u>n – s   x   DN   ptc   n   c – n</u>

Ps. 121:2   עזרי מעם יהוה עשה שמים וארץ   *f*

Ps. 124:8   עזרנו בשם יהוה עשה שמים וארץ   *g*

The first cola of *f* and *g* form a system: $\underline{\quad n - s \quad x \quad DN \quad}$

עָזְרִי מֵעִם יְהוָה Ps. 121:2a *h*

עָזְרֵנוּ בְּשֵׁם יְהוָה Ps. 124:8a *i*

Note that the x element does not represent a radical variation.

54

System: $\underline{\quad v \quad n \quad p - n \quad c - n \quad p - N \quad}$

יִשְׁפֹּט תֵּבֵל בְּצֶדֶק וְעַמִּים בֶּאֱמוּנָתוֹ Ps. 96:13 *a*

יִשְׁפֹּט תֵּבֵל בְּצֶדֶק וְעַמִּים בְּמֵישָׁרִים Ps. 98:9 *b*

(וְהוּא) יִשְׁפֹּט תֵּבֵל בְּצֶדֶק (יָדִין) לְאֻמִּים בְּמֵישָׁרִים Ps. 9:9 *c*

Note that *c* drops the conjunction but adds a verb in that position.

Also the system: $\underline{\quad v \quad n \quad p - n \quad}$

יָדִין לְאֻמִּים בְּמֵישָׁרִים Ps. 9:9b *d*

יָדִין עַמִּים בְּמֵישָׁרִים Ps. 96:10 *e*

Phrase *d* is the last colon of *c* and may be placed with *e* to form a system.

55

Four separate formulas follow, the last of which is only a possible formula because it occurs only once in poetry. They are found together in a number of places. Prose occurrences are included to show how widely these phrases have been used.

Formula i: $\quad adj + n \quad c - adj + n$

אֶרֶךְ אַפַּיִם וְרַב חֶסֶד Ps. 103:8 *a*

אֶרֶךְ אַפַּיִם וְרַב חֶסֶד Joel 2:13 *b*

אֶרֶךְ אַפַּיִם וְרַב חֶסֶד (וֶאֱמֶת) Ps. 86:15 *c*

Also in prose:

אֶרֶךְ אַפַּיִם וְרַב חֶסֶד Jon. 4:2 *d*

אֶרֶךְ אַפַּיִם וְרַב חֶסֶד (וֶאֱמֶת) Exod. 34:6 *e*

אֶרֶךְ אַפַּיִם וְרַב חֶסֶד Num. 14:18 *f*

Variation: <u>adj + n   c – adj + n</u>

Ps. 145:8   <u>ארך אפים וגדל חסד</u>   *g*

Formula ii: <u>adj   c – adj   DN</u>

Ps. 145:8   <u>חנון ורחום יהוה</u>   *h*

Ps. 111:4   <u>חנון ורחום יהוה</u>   *i*

Ps. 103:8   <u>רחום וחנון יהוה</u>   *j*

Note that in *j* the order of the first two words is reversed.

Variant: <u>adj   c – adj   pr</u>

Joel 2:13   <u>חנון ורחום הוא</u> (כי)   *k*

Possible variant: <u>adj   c – adj   c – adj</u>

Ps. 112:4   <u>חנון ורחום וצדיק</u>   *l*

Formula iii: <u>DN   adj   c – adj</u>

Ps. 86:15   <u>אל רחום וחנון</u> (ואתה אדני)   *m*

Also in prose:

Exod. 34:6   <u>אל רחום וחנון</u> (יהוה)   *n*

Jon. 4:2   <u>אל חנון ורחום</u> (אתה)   *o*

Note that in *o* the order of the last two words is reversed.

Possible formula iv: <u>c   ptc   p   n</u>

Joel 2:13   <u>ונחם על הרעה</u>   *p*

Also in prose: Jon. 4:2   <u>ונחם על הרעה</u>   *q*

These formulas are found together in the following combinations:

Ps. 86:15   <u>(ואתה אדני) אל רחום וחנון ארך אפים ורב חסד (ואמת)</u>   *r*

Ps. 103:8   <u>רחום וחנון יהוה ארך אפים ורב חסד</u>   *s*

Ps. 145:8   <u>חנון ורחום יהוה ארך אפים וגדל חסד</u>   *t*

Joel 2:13   <u>(כי) חנון ורחום הוא</u>   *u*

<u>ארך אפים ורב חסד ונחם על הרעה</u>

Also in prose:

אל רחום וחנון ארך אפים ורב חסד (ואמת) (יהוה)	Exod. 34:6	*v*
אל חנון ורחום ארך אפים ורב חסד ונחם על הרעה (אתה)	Jon. 4:2	*w*

Note that *r* is a combination of *m* and *c*; *s* of *j* and *a*; *t* of *h* and *g*; *u* of *k*, *b*, and *p*; *v* of *n* and *e*; and *w* of *c*, *d*, and *q*.

56

Formula: adj DN c – ptc adv

גדול יהוה ומהלל מאד	Ps. 48:2	*a*
גדול יהוה ומהלל מאד	Ps. 145:3	*b*
גדול יהוה ומהלל מאד (כי)	Ps. 96:4	*c*

57

System: n adj p n + n

מלך גדול על כל הארץ (כי יהוה עליון נורא)	Ps. 47:3	*a*
ו)מלך גדול על כל אלהים (כי אל גדול יהוה	Ps. 95:3	*b*

Formula: n p n + n

עליון על כל הארץ (מאד נעלית על כל אלהים) (כי אתה יהוה)	Ps. 97:9	*c*
עליון על כל הארץ (וידעו כי אתה שמך יהוה לבדך)	Ps. 83:19	*d*

System: ptc pr p n + n

נורא הוא על כל אלהים	Ps. 96:4	*e*
רם הוא על כל העמים (יהוה בציון גדול ו)	Ps. 99:2	*f*

Cf. also: ptc p n + n – s

נורא על כל סביביו (רבה ו)	Ps. 89:8	*g*

Phrase *g* is close to *e* and *f*, except that it lacks the pronoun.

Phrases *a*, *b*, *c*, *d*, *e*, and *f* have the same basic pattern of a nominal followed by a preposition and two nouns. The only lexical items common to all phrases are the preposition and the first noun following the preposition. The phrases enclosed in brackets each have interesting points of similarity with other phrases. For example, the phrases in *a*, *b*, *c*, and *d* each contain a clause beginning with the same particle and containing the same DN. The prepositional phrase in the bracketed part of *c* is the same as the prepositional phrase in *e*.

58

System: <u>DN</u>   v   x⋯⋯

יהוה מלך גאות לבש	Ps. 93:1	*a*
יהוה מלך תגל הארץ	Ps. 97:1	*b*
יהוה מלך ירגזו עמים	Ps. 99:1	*c*

Also: x⋯⋯   DN   v

אמרו בגוים יהוה מלך	Ps. 96:10	*d*

In *d* the x element precedes. This is another example of free substitution in which the constant element is only half a colon long and could be taken as a unit within the colon. See the comments to **20**. Note that the x element in *b* is the constant in **147**.

Cf. also the system: <u>DN</u>   x⋯⋯   n   c – n

יהוה מלך עולם ועד	Ps. 10:16	*e*
יהוה ימלך (ל)עולם ועד	Exod. 15:18	*f*

The x element in *e* is a noun but in *f* a verb.

59

System:

<u>impf 1 sg</u>   DN   p – n – s   impf 1 sg   p – DN – s   p – N – s

אשירה (ל)יהוה בחיי אזמרה לאלהי בעודי	Ps. 104:33	*a*
אהללה יהוה בחיי אזמרה לאלהי בעודי	Ps. 146:2	*b*

These are both full lines. Note that all the imperfects have the ending /-ā/.

Cf. also: <u>impf 1 sg – s</u>   p – n – s

(כן) אברכך בחיי	Ps. 63:5	*c*

Phrase *c* forms a system with the first cola of *a* and *b*. A suffix stands in *c* in place of the DN in the others.

60

System: impf 1   c – impf 1   p – N

אגילה ואשמחה בחסדך	Ps. 31:8 *a*
נגילה ונשמחה בו	Ps. 118:24 *b*
נגילה ונשמחה בישועתו	Is. 25:9 *c*

Variation: impf 1   c – impf 1   p – N

(ו)נרננה ונשמחה בכל ימינו	Ps. 90:14 *d*

Also: impf 1   c – impf 1   p – N

אשמחה ואעלצה בך	Ps. 9:3 *e*

Phrase *e* is a possible variation. The first verb is lexically the same as the second verbs in *a*, *b*, and *c*.

Cf. also: impf 3 pl   c – impf 3 pl   p – N

ישישו וישמחו בך	Ps. 40:17 *f*

Phrase *f* is a possible variation in the third person.

61

System: V   n + n – s

אספרה כל נפלאותיך	Ps. 9:2 *a*
(למען) אספרה כל תהלתיך	Ps. 9:15 *b*
(ול)ספר כל נפלאותיך	Ps. 26:7 *c*
(ל)ספר כל מלאכותיך	Ps. 73:28 *d*

62

System: inter   v   x   inter   DN – s

למה יאמרו הגוים איה אלהיהם	Ps. 79:10 *a*
למה יאמרו הגוים איה (נא) אלהיהם	Ps. 115:2 *b*
למה יאמרו בעמים איה אלהיהם	Joel 2:17 *c*

The x element in *a* and *b* is a noun but in *c* a prepositional phrase.

63

System: $\underline{V}\ \underline{\ \ \ \ }\ \underline{p}-\underline{n}+\underline{n}-\underline{s}$

(ו)ארנן לבקר חסדך	Ps. 59:17	*a*
שבענו בבקר חסדך	Ps. 90:14	*b*
(ל)הגיד בבקר חסדך	Ps. 92:3	*c*
השמיעני בבקר חסדך	Ps. 143:8	*d*

Note that the verbal may be a verb as in *a*, a verb with suffix as in *b* and *d*, or a verbal noun as in *c*.

64

System: $\underline{v}\ \underline{\ \ \ N\ \ \ }\ \underline{p}-\underline{n}+\underline{n}-\underline{s}$

אודך בכל לבי	Ps. 138:1	*a*
אודך (אדני אלהי) בכל לבבי	Ps. 86:12	*b*
אודה יהוה בכל לבי	Ps. 9:2	*c*
אודה יהוה בכל לבב	Ps. 111:1	*d*

Note that phrase *d* does not have a suffix on the last noun. The nominal is a suffix in *a* and *b* but a DN in *c* and *d*.

Cf. also the system: $\underline{v}-\underline{s}\ \ \ \underline{p}-\underline{N}$

אודך בקהל רב	Ps. 35:18	*e*
(ו)אודך בכנור	Ps. 43:4	*f*
אודך בעמים (אדני)	Ps. 57:10	*g*
(על כן) אודך בגוים (יהוה)	Ps. 18:50	*h*
(גם אני) אודך בכלי נבל	Ps. 71:22	*i*

These two systems have been treated together because they have the same general pattern of verb–nominal–preposition–nominal and the verb and preposition is the same in each. One may be a variant of the other.

65

System: p   n   rel   v

בדרך זו תלך	Ps. 32:8	a
בארח זו אהלך	Ps. 142:4	b

Variant: n   rel   v

(הודיעני) דרך זו אלך	Ps. 143:8	c

The variant has a verb in the place where a preposition stands in the others.

66

System: x   N   p – s

וידבר עמים תחתי	Ps. 18:48	a
ידבר עמים תחתינו	Ps. 47:4	b
הרודד עמי תחתי	Ps. 144:2	c

Note that the variation in the x element is not great. This element is a verb in *a* and *b* but a participle in *c*. A participle can take verbal modifiers.

67

System: n   p – n – s   impf

(ו)אש מפיו תאכל	Ps. 18:9	a
אש לפניו תאכל	Ps. 50:3	b
אש לפניו תלך	Ps. 97:3	c

68

System: part   part   n – s   impf 3 pl

כי הנה רחקיך יאבדו	Ps. 73:27	a
כי הנה אויביך יהמיון	Ps. 83:3	b
כי הנה איביך (יהוה) כי הנה איביך יאבדו	Ps. 92:10	c

Phrase *c* has been expanded by a repetition of the two particles and the noun with suffix. A DN has also been added.

69

Formula:	n – s	c – n	DN	c – v	p – s	p – n		

עזי וזמרת יה ויהי לי לישועה	Ps. 118:14	*a*
עזי וזמרת יה ויהי לי לישועה	Exod. 15:2	*b*
(כי) עזי וזמרת יה (יהוה) ויהי לי לישועה	Is. 12:2	*c*

70

System:	v	p – n	n – s		

זכר לעולם בריתו	Ps. 105:8	*a*
יזכר לעולם בריתו	Ps. 111:5	*b*
צוה לעולם בריתו	Ps. 111:9	*c*

71

Formula:	v	part	n	

יאמר נא ישראל	Ps. 118:2	*a*
יאמר נא ישראל	Ps. 124:1	*b*
יאמר נא ישראל	Ps. 129:1	*c*

72

Formula:

v	p – DN	part	adj	part	p – n	n – s	

הודו ליהוה כי טוב כי לעולם חסדו	Ps. 106:1

This phrase is also the first line in Pss. 107, 118, and 136, and the last line in Ps. 118. The last half of this line is found as a refrain in Ps. 118 five times and in Ps. 136 twenty-six times. Thus while the line and its last half fit the definition of a formula, they seem to be used in special ways. It is difficult to decide whether this is a formula or not.

73

System: _ _impv_ _ _p_ _ _n_–_s_ _

Ps. 142:7   הַקְשִׁיבָה אֶל רִנָּתִי   *a*

Ps. 143:1   הַאֲזִינָה אֶל תַּחֲנוּנַי   *b*

Common lexical items are the preposition and the suffix on the noun. Although the verbs are from different roots, they have the same vowel pattern and have a similar meaning. Thus they are virtual lexical constants.

Cf. also: _ _impv_ _ _p_–_N_–_s_ _

Ps. 54:4   הַאֲזִינָה לְאִמְרֵי פִי   *c*

This could be related. Note that the verb is the same as the one in *b*. It is, however, only a possible variant.

74

System: _ _impv_–_s_ _ _p_–_N_ _ _p_ _ _n_–_s_ _

Ps. 5:9   (יהוה) נְחֵנִי בְצִדְקָתֶךָ לְמַעַן שׁוֹרְרָי   *a*

Ps. 27:11   (וּ)נְחֵנִי בְּאֹרַח מִישׁוֹר לְמַעַן שׁוֹרְרָי   *b*

75

System: _ _impv_ _ _p_–_n_ _ _n_–_s_ _

Ps. 22:21   הַצִּילָה מֵחֶרֶב נַפְשִׁי   *a*

Ps. 142:8   הוֹצִיאָה מִמַּסְגֵּר נַפְשִׁי   *b*

The verbs both have a similar vowel pattern and might be considered virtual lexical constants.

Variation in impf: _ _impf_ _ _p_–_n_ _ _n_–_s_ _

Ps. 143:11   (בְצִדְקָתֶךָ) תּוֹצִיא מִצָּרָה נַפְשִׁי   *c*

Note that the verbs in *b* and *c* are lexically the same.

76

System: <u>p – n + n</u> <u>impf 2 m sg – s</u>

מאיש חמס תצילני   Ps. 18:49   *a*

מאיש חמסים תנצרני   Ps. 140:2.5   *b*

77

System: <u>impv – s</u>   <u>p – n + n</u>

(אלהי) פלטני מיד רשע   Ps. 71:4   *a*

שמרני (יהוה) מידי רשע   Ps. 140:5   *b*

Note that a DN precedes the verb in *a* and follows in *b*.

78

System: <u>impv – s</u>   <u>p – n – s</u>

חנני (אלהים) כחסדך   Ps. 51:3   *a*

חנני כאמרתך   Ps. 119:58   *b*

79

Formula: <u>impv – s   DN   impv – s</u>

חנני אלהים חנני   Ps. 57:2   *a*

חננו יהוה חננו   Ps. 123:3   *b*

80

Formula: <u>impv   DN   c – impv</u>

ראה יהוה והביטה   Lam. 1:11   *a*

ראה יהוה והביטה   Lam. 2:20   *b*

81

System:
<u>DN   neg   p – n – s   v – s   c – p – n – s   v – s</u>

יהוה אל באפך תוכיחני ו(אל) בחמתך תיסרני   Ps. 6:2   *a*

יהוה אל בקצפך תוכיחני ובחמתך תיסרני   Ps. 38:2   *b*

82

System: <u>neg   v – s   p – n   n – s</u>

אל תתנני בנפש צרי   Ps. 27:12   *a*

(ו)אל תתנהו בנפש איביו   Ps. 41:3   *b*

83

System: <u>neg   v – s   N</u>

אל תעזבני יהוה   Ps. 38:22   *a*

(אל תטשני ו)אל תעזבני אלהי ישעי   Ps. 27:9   *b*

Note that *b* is a full line.

Cf. also: <u>neg   v – s   x</u>

אל תעזבני עד מאד   Ps. 119:8   *c*

Possible variation with free substitution in last position.

Also: <u>x   neg   v – s</u>

ככלות כחי אל תעזבני   Ps. 71:9   *d*

אלהים אל תעזבני   Ps. 71:18   *e*

Here the x element precedes. For a similar constant element and free substitution, see **23**.

84

System: <u>v   p – s   n – s</u>

ותנחת עלי ידך   Ps. 38:3   *a*

תכבד עלי ידך   Ps. 32:4   *b*

85

System: <u>v   n   p   n</u>

אפפו(ני) מים עד נפש   Jon. 2:6   *a*

(כי) באו מים עד נפש   Ps. 69:2   *b*

86

Formula: n + n – s   c – n – s   p – s   v

כל מבשריך וגליך עלי עברו	Ps. 42:8	a
כל מבשריך וגליך עלי עברו	Jon. 2:4	b

This is a full line.

87

System: c – n – s   p – s   adv

ומכאובי נגדי תמיד	Ps. 38:18	a
וחטאתי נגדי תמיד	Ps. 51:5	b

88

System: v   p – n   n – s

עששה מכעס עיני	Ps. 6:8	a
עששה בכעס עיני (נפשי ובטני)	Ps. 31:10	b

89

System: n – s   v   p – n – s

לבי יחיל בקרבי	Ps. 55:5	a
(ו)לבי חלל בקרבי	Ps. 109:22	b

90

System: part   v   p – n   n – s

כי כלו ביגון חיי	Ps. 31:11	a
כי כלו בעשן ימי	Ps. 102:4	b

91

Formula: n + n   v   n – s

פלגי מים ירדו עיני	Ps. 119:136	a
פלגי מים תרד עיני	Lam. 3:48	b

92

System: <u>v   n   n – s</u>   <u>v   p – n   n – s</u>

Ps. 7:6   <u>ירדף אויב נפשי</u> (<u>וישג ו</u>)<u>ירמס לארץ חיַי</u>   *a*

Ps. 143:3   (כי) <u>רדף אויב נפשי דכא לארץ חיתי</u>   *b*

Phrase *a* has a verb and two conjunctions not in *b*. The final nouns with suffix in each are different forms of the same root and are virtually lexical constants.

93

Formula: <u>V   p – s   n – s</u>

Ps. 35:16   <u>חרק עלי שנימו</u>   *a*

Ps. 37:12   (ו)<u>חרק עליו שניו</u>   *b*

The variants are different forms of the verb, an infinitive absolute in *a* and a participle in *b*, and different persons in the suffixes. These changes are permitted in formulas.

94

Formula: <u>V   part   part</u>

Ps. 35:21   <u>אמרו האח האח</u>   *a*

Ps. 40:16   <u>האמרים</u> (<u>לי</u>) <u>האח האח</u>   *b*

95

Formula: <u>p – n   n   p – s</u>

Ps. 59:17   (ומנוס) <u>ביום צר לי</u>   *a*

Ps. 102:3   <u>ביום צר לי</u>   *b*

96

Formula: <u>part   v   adv</u>

Ps. 79:8   <u>כי דלונו מאד</u>   *a*

Ps. 142:7   <u>כי דלותי מאד</u>   *b*

97

Formula: <u>part pr n – s</u>

<u>כי אני עבדך</u> Ps. 116:16   *a*

<u>כי אני עבדך</u> Ps. 143:12   *b*

98

System: <u>v n p – n</u>

<u>זכרתי ימים מקדם</u> Ps. 143:5   *a*

<u>השבתי ימים מקדם</u> Ps. 77:6   *b*

Formula: <u>v p – n + n – s</u>

<u>הגיתי בכל פעלך</u> Ps. 143:5   *c*

(ו)<u>הגיתי בכל פעלך</u> Ps. 77:13   *d*

Phrases *a* and *c* make the first two cola of a tricola line and *b* and *d* are in the same psalm.

99

Formula: <u>ptc n + n</u>

(שנאתי ה)<u>שמרים הבלי שוא</u> Ps. 31:7   *a*

(מ)<u>שמרים הבלי שוא</u> Jon. 2:9   *b*

100

System: <u>p – n rel v x</u>

<u>ברשת זו טמנו נלכדה רגלם</u> Ps. 9:16   *a*

תוציאני <u>מרשת זו טמנו</u> (לי) Ps. 31:5   *b*

Note that the x element precedes in one and follows in the other.

101

System: <u>impf 1 sg p – DN part x</u>

<u>אשירה ליהוה כי גמל עלי</u> Ps. 13:6   *a*

<u>אשירה ליהוה כי גאה גאה</u> Exod. 15:1   *b*

Both imperfects have an /-ā/ ending. For a similar example of free substitution, see **16** and the comments made there.

102

Formula: <u>impf 1 sg   c – impf 1 sg</u>

<u>אשירה ואזמרה</u> (ליהוה)	Ps. 27:6	*a*
<u>אשירה ואזמרה</u>	Ps. 57:8	*b*

Note that the verbs have an /-ā/ ending.

103

System: <u>p – N   v   p – s</u>

<u>בנדבה אזבחה לך</u>	Ps. 54:8	*a*
(ואני) <u>בקול תדה אזבחה לך</u>	Jon. 2:10	*b*

104

System: <u>impf 1 sg   n – s   part   n</u>

(ו)<u>אקוה שמך כי טוב</u>	Ps. 52:11	*a*
<u>אודה שמך</u> (יהוה) <u>כי טוב</u>	Ps. 54:8	*b*

105

System: <u>p – n   n – s   v</u>

<u>במעשי ידיך ארנן</u>	Ps. 92:5	*a*
<u>במעשה ידיך אשוחח</u>	Ps. 143:5	*b*

106

Formula: <u>v   p – n – s</u>

(הורני יהוה דרכך) <u>אהלך באמתך</u>	Ps. 86:11	*a*
(ו)<u>התהלכתי באמתך</u>	Ps. 26:3	*b*

Example *a* appears to form a part of a colon only. The other part of the colon is found as a formula in **13**.

107

Formula: <u>v   p – n   n – s</u>

<u>ארחץ בנקיון כפי</u>	Ps. 26:6	*a*
(ו)<u>ארחץ בנקיון כפי</u>	Ps. 73:13	*b*

108

Formula: $\underline{\quad v \qquad p \qquad n + n - s \quad}$

אשתחוה אל היכל קדשך	Ps. 5:8	*a*
אשתחוה אל היכל קדשך	Ps. 138:2	*b*

109

System: $\underline{\quad v \qquad DN \qquad x \quad}$

שובה יהוה חלצה נפשי	Ps. 6:5	*a*
שובה יהוה עד מתי	Ps. 90:13	*b*

The x element of *a* is in turn a member of the system in **17**. Here is another example in which it appears that a colon has been formed from two smaller elements which are constants. See the comments to **20**.

110

System:

$\underline{\quad p \qquad inter \qquad DN \qquad v \qquad p-n \qquad v \qquad p-s \qquad n+n-s \quad}$

עד מה יהוה תאנף לנצח תבער כמו אש קנאתך	Ps. 79:5	*a*
עד מה יהוה תסתר לנצח תבער כמו אש חמתך	Ps. 89:47	*b*

111

System: $\underline{\quad v \qquad n \qquad p-n-s \qquad n \qquad c-n \qquad p-n-s \quad}$

הויינו חרפה לשכנינו לעג וקלס לסביבותינו	Ps. 79:4	*a*
תשימנו חרפה לשכנינו לעג וקלס לסביבותינו	Ps. 44:14	*b*

Cf. also:

היה חרפה לשכניו	Ps. 89:42	*c*

Phrase *c* is a possible variation of the first colon of the system of *a* and *b*.

112

System: <u>impv   x   c – impv</u>
              ....

הבט משמים וראה   Ps. 80:15   *a*
....

הביט ימין וראה   Ps. 142:5   *b*
....

הבט משמים וראה   Is. 63:15   *c*
....

Example *c* does not come from psalm literature. One is tempted to consider the x element in *b* a corruption of the preposition with noun of *a* and *c*. There is, however, no evidence to support this.

113

Formula: <u>impv   n + DN</u>

הללו עבדי יהוה   Ps. 113:1a   *a*

הללו עבדי יהוה   Ps. 135:1b   *b*

Also the formula: <u>impv   part   n – DN</u>

הללו את שם יהוה   Ps. 113:1b   *c*

הללו את שם יהוה   Ps. 135:1a   *d*

Phrases *a* and *c* form a line, as do *d* and *b*.

114

System: <u>impv   DN   p – DN</u>

רננו צדיקים ביהוה   Ps. 33:1   *a*

שמחו צדיקים ביהוה   Ps. 97:12   *b*

115

System: <u>impv   part   DN   p – n</u>

עבדו את יהוה ביראה   Ps. 2:11   *a*

עבדו את יהוה בשמחה   Ps. 100:1   *b*

116

Formula: <u>c – impv pl</u>   <u>p – n + n – s</u>

<u>והודו לזכר קדשו</u>	Ps. 30:5	*a*
<u>והודו לזכר קדשו</u>	Ps. 97:12	*b*

117

System: <u>impv</u>   <u>impv</u>   <u>n + DN</u>

<u>לכו חֲזוּ מפעלות יהוה</u>	Ps. 46:9	*a*
<u>לכו (וּ)רְאוּ מפעלות אלהים</u>	Ps. 66:5	*b*

118

Formula: <u>p – n + n</u>   <u>v</u>   <u>p – s</u>

<u>בנבל עשור זמרו לו</u>	Ps. 33:2	*a*
<u>בנבל עשור אזמרה לך</u>	Ps. 144:9	*b*

The variation of person in the suffix and form of the verb is permitted within the formula.

119

Formula: <u>v</u>   <u>p – n + n – s</u>

<u>(ו)השתחוו להדם רגליו</u>	Ps. 99:5	*a*
<u>נשתחוה להדם רגליו</u>	Ps. 132:7	*b*

120

System: <u>n – s</u>   <u>ptc</u>   <u>p – n</u>

<u>(ו)צִדְקָתוֹ עמדת לעד</u>	Ps. 111:3	*a*
<u>תהלתו עמדת לעד</u>	Ps. 111:10	*b*
<u>(ו)צִדְקָתוֹ עמדת לעד</u>	Ps. 112:3	*c*
<u>צדקתו עמדת לעד</u>	Ps. 112:9	*d*

Note further that the noun with suffix is constant in *a*, *c*, and *d*.

121

System: <u>N</u> <u>p – n + n</u>

עֶלְיוֹן לְמַלְכֵי אֶרֶץ Ps. 89:28 *a*

נוֹרָא לְמַלְכֵי אֶרֶץ Ps. 76:13 *b*

Cf. **57c** and *d*.

122

Formula: <u>ptc n – s p – n</u>

מְלַמֵּד יָדַי לַמִּלְחָמָה Ps. 18:35 *a*

הַמְלַמֵּד יָדַי (לִקְרָב אֶצְבְּעוֹתַי) לַמִּלְחָמָה Ps. 144:1 *b*

Note the expansion to a full line in *b*.

123

System: <u>impv part pr DN</u>

דְּעוּ כִּי (יְהוָה) הוּא אֱלֹהִים Ps. 100:3 *a*

(הַרְפּוּ וְ)דְעוּ כִּי אָנֹכִי אֱלֹהִים Ps. 46:11 *b*

Both phrases have an added element. Phrase *a* has a DN and phrase *b* has expanded the line by adding another verb.

124

System: <u>ptc n p – N</u>

נֹתֵן לֶחֶם לְכָל בָּשָׂר Ps. 136:25 *a*

נֹתֵן לֶחֶם לָרְעֵבִים Ps. 146:7 *b*

125

Formula: <u>n rel v v</u>

כֹּל אֲשֶׁר חָפֵץ עָשָׂה Ps. 115:3 *a*

כֹּל אֲשֶׁר חָפֵץ (יְהוָה) עָשָׂה Ps. 135:6 *b*

126

System: pr   DN   p – n   v   n – s   p – n   c – n

(ו)אתה יהוה לעולם תשב (ו)זכרך לדר ודר	Ps. 102:13	*a*
אתה יהוה לעולם תשב כסאך לדר ודור	Lam. 5:19	*b*

127

Formula: n   c – n + p – s

(ליהוה הארץ ומלואה) תבל וישבי בה	Ps. 24:1	*a*
(ירעם הים ומלאו) תבל וישבי בה	Ps. 98:7	*b*

The first colon of each has been included in brackets because it
contains a lexical constant, the conjunction followed by the noun
with suffix.

Cf. also the formula: v   n   c – n – s

ירעם הים ומלאו	Ps. 98:7	*c*
ירעם הים ומלאו	Ps. 96:11	*d*

The first part of *b* is identical with a colon in Ps. 96:11.

128

System: inter   v   n – s   DN

מה גדלו מעשיך יהוה	Ps. 92:6	*a*
מה רבו מעשיך יהוה	Ps. 104:24	*b*

129

Formula: part   DN   ptc

כי אלהים שפט (הוא)	Ps. 50:6	*a*
כי אלהים שפט	Ps. 75:8	*b*

130

System: part   n   v

כִּי נִפְלָאוֹת עָשָׂה   Ps. 98:1   *a*

כִּי גֵאוּת עָשָׂה   Is. 12:5   *b*

Note that both nouns, although lexically different, are feminine plural.

131

System: N   v   n

חֶסֶד יהוה מָלְאָה הָאָרֶץ   Ps. 33:5   *a*

חַסְדְּךָ (יהוה) מָלְאָה הָאָרֶץ   Ps. 119:64   *b*

In *a* the nominal is a noun in a bound construction to a DN while it is a noun with a suffix in *b*. Phrase *b* has added a DN as a vocative.

132

Formula: n   c – n   n + n – s

צֶדֶק וּמִשְׁפָּט מְכוֹן כִּסְאָךְ   Ps. 89:15   *a*

צֶדֶק וּמִשְׁפָּט מְכוֹן כִּסְאוֹ   Ps. 97:2   *b*

The only variation is a change of person in the suffix.

133

Formula: part   v   n   neg   v

אַף תִּכּוֹן תֵּבֵל בַּל תִּמּוֹט   Ps. 93:1   *a*

אַף תִּכּוֹן תֵּבֵל בַּל תִּמּוֹט   Ps. 96:10   *b*

134

System: V   p   n + n

(וַ)יֵּדֶא עַל כַּנְפֵי רוּחַ   Ps. 18:11   *a*

הַמְהַלֵּךְ עַל כַּנְפֵי רוּחַ   Ps. 104:3   *b*

The participle in *b* has been considered a verbal here because it is modified by a prepositional phrase.

135

Formula: <u>p – DN   part   v   p – vn   n</u>

<u>לפני יהוה כי בא לשפט הארץ</u>   Ps. 98:9   *a*

<u>לפני יהוה כי בא (כי בא) לשפט הארץ</u>   Ps. 96:13   *b*

The added element in *b* could be an expansion or a case of dittography.

136

Formula: <u>n – s   c – n – s   pr</u>

<u>עזרנו ומגננו הוא</u>   Ps. 33:20   *a*

<u>עזרם ומגנם הוא</u>   Ps. 115: 9.10.11   *b*

The occurrences listed in *b* are a refrain. The only variation is a change of person in the suffix.

137

Formula: <u>v   n   n – s</u>

<u>(ו)יגידו שמים צדקו</u>   Ps. 50:6   *a*

<u>הגידו השמים צדקו</u>   Ps. 97:6   *b*

138

Formula: <u>DN   p – n + n – s</u>

<u>יהוה בהיכל קדשו</u>   Ps. 11:4   *a*

<u>(ו)יהוה בהיכל קדשו</u>   Hab. 2:20   *b*

139

System: <u>n   DN   p – N</u>

<u>קרוב יהוה לנשברי לב</u>   Ps. 34:19   *a*

<u>קרוב יהוה לכל קראיו</u>   Ps. 145:18   *b*

140

System: x   neg   v   inter   v   p – s   n

יהוה לי לא אירא מה יעשה לי אדם	Ps. 118:6	*a*
באלהים בטחתי לא אירא מה יעשה בשר לי	Ps. 56:5	*b*
באלהים בטחתי לא אירא מה יעשה אדם לי	Ps. 56:12	*c*

Note that the phrase is used in Ps. 56 as a refrain. Here the order of the last two items is reversed.

Also the system: p – DN   v   neg   impf 1 sg

באלהים בטחתי לא אירא	Ps. 56:5	*d*
באלהים בטחתי לא אירא	Ps. 56:12	*e*
(ו)ביהוה בטחתי לא אמעד	Ps. 26:1	*f*

The first part of *b* forms a system with the first part of *c* and another phrase.

141

Formula: v   p – n   c – v

יגע בהרים ויעשנו	Ps. 104:32	*a*
גע בהרים ויעשנו	Ps. 144:5	*b*

142

System: v   n   n   v   c – v   n

האירו ברקים תבל רגזה ותרעש הארץ	Ps. 77:19	*a*
האירו ברק(יו) תבל ראתה ותחל הארץ	Ps. 97:4	*b*

Also the system: v   c – v   n

(ו)תגעש ותרעש הארץ	Ps. 18:8	*c*
רגזה ותרעש הארץ	Ps. 77:19	*d*
ראתה ותחל הארץ	Ps. 97:4	*e*

The last cola of *a* and *b* form a system with another phrase. Note that in *c* and *d* the second verb is a lexical constant.

143

Formula: impv   p   DN

קוה אל יהוה (חזק ויאמץ לבך) וקוה אל יהוה   Ps. 27:14   *a*

קוה אל יהוה   Ps. 37:34   *b*

Note that in *a* the formula is repeated. The phrase in brackets appears as a formula in **145**.

144

Formula: impv   p – n   c – impv   n

סור מרע ועשה טוב   Ps. 34:15   *a*

סור מרע ועשה טוב   Ps. 37:27   *b*

145

Formula: impv   c – v   n – s

חזק ויאמץ לבך   Ps. 27:14   *a*

חזקו ויאמץ לבבכם   Ps. 31:25   *b*

Phrase *b* is expressed in the plural.

146

Formula: v – s   DN   p – n

יברכך יהוה מציון   Ps. 128:5   *a*

יברכך יהוה מציון   Ps. 134:3   *b*

147

System: x   v   n

ישמחו השמים (ו)תגל הארץ   Ps. 96:11   *a*

יהוה מלך תגל הארץ   Ps. 97:1   *b*

For comments on the x element, see **20**. Note that the x element in *b* appears as a formula in **58**.

148

Formula: <u>v</u>   <u>adv</u>   <u>v</u>   <u>DN</u>

(ירנו וישמחו חפצי צדקי)   Ps. 35:27   *a*

ו)יאמרו תמיד יגדל יהוה (החפץ שלום עבדו)

(ישישו וישמחו בך כל מבקשיך)   Ps. 40:17   *b*

יאמרו תמיד יגדל יהוה (אהבי תשועתך)

In *a* the lines have been divided differently than in the text of *Biblica Hebraica* prepared by F. Buhl. In the Buhl text, the first two words of the formula are placed at the end of the first line. The first lines do not have a common pattern but both begin with two imperfects, the second of which is the same.

149

Formula: <u>v</u>   <u>n + n</u>   <u>p</u>   <u>n – s</u>

(ישמח הר ציון)   Ps. 48:12   *a*

תגלנה בנות יהודה למען משפטיך

(שמעה ותשמח ציון) ותגלנה בנות יהודה   Ps. 97:8   *b*

למען משפטיך (יהוה)

The first three words of both *a* and *b* are not included in the formula because they have no common pattern. However, they were written down with the others because they contain common lexical items.

150

System: <u>c – v</u>   <u>p – s</u>   <u>n + n – s</u>

(ותסך עלימו) ויעלצו בך אהבי שמך   Ps. 5:12   *a*

ויבטחו בך יודעי שמך   Ps. 9:11   *b*

Phrase *a* is a full line but *b* is a colon.

151

Formula: <u>v</u>   <u>n</u>   <u>p</u>   <u>DN</u>

יחל ישראל אל יהוה   Ps. 130:7   *a*

יחל ישראל אל יהוה   Ps. 131:3   *b*

152

Formula: p – n + n   p   n – s

ממזרח שמש עד מבאו	Ps. 50:1	*a*
ממזרח שמש עד מבואו	Ps. 113:3	*b*

153

Formula: ptc p – n – s

(ל)מיחלים לחסדו	Ps. 33:18	*a*
(את) המיחלים לחסדו	Ps. 147:11	*b*

154

Formula: neg   v   p – vn   n – s

(ו)לא נתן למוט רגלנו	Ps. 66:9	*a*
אל יתן למוט רגלך	Ps. 121:3	*b*

There are variations in the form of the verb and the person of the suffix.

155

System: n   perf 3 sg   p – s   n – s

רבת שכנה לה נפשי	Ps. 120:6	*a*
רבת שבעה לה נפשנו	Ps. 123:4	*b*

156

System: impf 3 m sg – s   part   v   p – s

יחלצני כי חפץ בי	Ps. 18:20	*a*
יצילהו כי חפץ בו	Ps. 22:9	*b*

157

Formula: n – s   v   p – s

אבותינו ספרו לנו	Ps. 44:2	*a*
(ו)אבותינו ספרו לנו	Ps. 78:3	*b*

158

Formula: ptc   p – n + DN

עמדים בבית יהוה(ה)   Ps. 134:1   *a*

עמדים בבית יהוה(ש)   Ps. 135:2   *b*

159

Formula: c   neg   v   p – n – s

ולא תצא בצבאותינו   Ps. 44:10   *a*

ולא תצא (אלהים) בצבאותינו   Ps. 60:12   *b*

160

Formula: V   p – n   n – s

הכרית מארץ זכרם(ל)   Ps. 34:17   *a*

יכרית מארץ זכרם(ו)   Ps. 109:15   *b*

161

System: v   n   c – v

יראו רבים וייראו   Ps. 40:4   *a*

יראו צדיקים וייראו(ו)   Ps. 52:8   *b*

162

Formula: v   n – s   c – v   p – s

שמע עמי ואעידה בך   Ps. 81:9   *a*

שמעה עמי (ואדברה ישראל) ואעידה בך   Ps. 50:7   *b*

Note the expansion to a full line in *b*.

In the following, one of the phrases comes from outside psalm literature.

163

Formula: part   v   DN   n – s   c – p   n – s   v

כי ידין יהוה עמו ועל עבדיו יתנחם   Ps. 135:14   *a*

כי ידין יהוה עמו ועל עבדיו יתנחם   Dt. 32:36   *b*

7

164

Formula: <u>adv   v   v   DN</u>

עתה אקום יאמר יהוה   Ps. 12:6 *a*

עתה אקום יאמר יהוה   Is. 33:10 *b*

165

Formula: <u>v   n   p − n + n</u>

ישם מדבר לאגם מים   Ps. 107:35 *a*

אשים מדבר לאגם מים   Is. 41:18 *b*

166

Formula: <u>c − n + n   v</u>

(כי שבר דלתות נחשת) ובריחי ברזל גדע   Ps. 107:16 *a*

(דלתות נחושה אשבר) ובריחי ברזל אגדע   Is. 45:2 *b*

Note that the first cola of *a* and *b* contain the same or similar lexical items but in a different order. See comments to **170**.

167

Formula: <u>v   n + n + n   part   n + DN − s</u>

ראו כל אפסי ארץ את ישועת אלהינו   Ps. 98:3 *a*

(ו)ראו כל אפסי ארץ את ישועת אלהינו   Is. 52:10 *b*

168

Formula: <u>part   v   n + n   n   p − n</u>

כי שמעתי דבת רבים מגור מסביב   Ps. 31:14 *a*

כי שמעתי דבת רבים מגור מסביב   Jer. 20:10 *b*

169

System: n + DN   n   n   pr   p – n   p – s

אמרת יהוה צרופה מגן הוא ל(כל) החסים בו   Ps. 18:31   *a*

(כל) אמרת אלוה צרופה מגן הוא לחסים בו   Prov. 30:5   *b*

The following phrases ought to be considered but they contain problems, and so are listed separately.

170

Possibly related: impv – s   p – n   p – n + n

הושיבני במחשבים כמתי עולם   Ps. 143:3   *a*

במחשבים הושיבני כמתי עולם   Lam. 3:6   *b*

The items are the same but the order is different. In *a* the imperative comes first but in *b* the prepositional phrase precedes. There are a few examples of this sort of phenomenon in which the same or similar elements are found in a different order. See **171**, **173**, and **175**. There are, however, not enough examples to indicate definitely that this sort of variation would be a normal one for an oral poet to make. These phrases appear to be related because of common forms and lexical items, but the nature of this relationship cannot be determined.

171

Possibly related: c – v   DN   p – n   p – s

ויהי יהוה למשען לי   Ps. 18:19   *a*

ויהי יהוה לי למשגב   Ps. 94:22   *b*

See the comments to **170**.

Cf. also: c – v   DN   n   p – N

ויהי יהוה משגב לדך   Ps. 9:10   *c*

In *c* the first preposition is lacking and a noun stands in place of the suffix. Note that the first noun is the same as the noun in *b*.

172

Possible formula: v   n   c – v

Ps. 18:10   (ו)יט שמים וירד   *a*

Ps. 144:5   (יהוה) הט שמיך ותרד   *b*

The verbs in *a* are in the perfect aspect, the third person. The verbs in *b* are in the imperative and the imperfect, the second person.

173

Possibly related: v , p – n   p – s ,   p – DN ,   c – v

Jon. 2:3   קראתי מצרה לי אל יהוה ויענני   *a*

Ps. 120:1   אל יהוה בצרתה לי קראתי ויענני   *b*

These two phrases have no common pattern but the elements are the same apart from the preposition with the noun. See the comments to **170**.

174

Possibly related: x   c – v   x   c – v

Ps. 18:15   וישלח חציו ויפיצם וברקים רב ויהמם   *a*

Ps. 144:6   ברוק ברק ותפיצם שלח חציך ותהמם   *b*

The first x element in *a* has lexical and structural similarities to the second x element in *b*. The second x element in *a* has a lexical similarity to the first x element in *b*.

175

Possibly related: n – s ,   v   n – s ,   n + n

Ps. 35:28   (ו)לשוני תהגה צדקך כל היום (תהלתך)   *a*

Ps. 71:24   (גם) לשוני כל היום תהגה צדקתך   *b*

There is no common pattern because the elements appear in a different order. See the comments to **170**.

The following are two special cases.

176

Ps. 18:3   יהוה סלעי ומצודתי ומפלטי אלי צורי אחסה בו
מגני וקרן ישעי משגבי

Ps. 144:2   חסדי ומצודתי משגבי ומפלטי לי
מגני ובו חסיתי

Ps. 91:2   אמר ליהוה מחסי ומצודתי אלהי אבטח בו

Ps. 28:7   יהוה עזי ומגני בו בטח לבי

There is no common pattern but each has a series of nouns with first person singular suffixes and each has a verb with a preposition with suffix either before or after it.

177

Ps. 77:18   זרמו מים עבות קול נתנו שחקים אף <u>חצציך יתהלכו</u>

Hab. 3:10.11   זרם מים עבר נתן תהום קולו
רום ידיהו נשא שמש ירח עמד זבלה
לאור <u>חציך יהלכו</u>

These phrases have no pattern of any significance but they have common lexical items in almost the same order. These have been underlined.

Three other characteristics of oral style very closely related to the use of formulas and formulaic phrases were discussed earlier in Chapter 2: runs, adding style, and contradictions. Something can be said on each of these points with regard to the Hebrew poetry of the biblical psalms.

Runs are groups of formulas or formulaic phrases that often appear together in the same or slightly different order. There are not many groups of phrases among the biblical psalms that fit this description but the few that do occur are worth recording. In the following list the common material is indicated by the same system of underlining already used for the formulas and formulaic phrases. Some of the phrases among the instances of possible runs to be presented have already been recorded as examples of formulas and formulaic phrases. These will be noted.

The most promising examples of runs are:

A

Ps. 22:20   (ואתה) יהוה אל תרחק אילותי לעזרתי חושה

Ps. 38:22.23   אל תעזבני יהוה אלהי אל תרחק ממני

חושה לעזרתי אדני (תשועתי)

Ps. 71:12   אלהים אל תרחק ממני אלהי לעזרתי חישה

These phrases have been listed separately in **19** and **21**.

B

Ps. 69:18   (ו)אל תסתר פניך מעבדך כי צר לי מהר ע=ני

Ps. 102:3   אל תסתר פניך ממני ביום צר לי

הטה אלי אזנך ביום אקרא מהר עָנֵני

Ps. 143:7   מהר עָנֵני יהוה כלתה רוחי

אל תסתר פניך ממני ונמשלתי עם ירדי בור

The two underlined phrases appearing in each are listed separately in **20** and **21**. Note that the phrases appear in a different order in the last example.

Examples **A** and **B** both contain three occurrences, but only two phrases are involved in each instance.

The remaining examples contain groups of phrases that occur only twice. These may be divided into two classes. In the first place, there are possible runs in which most of the phrases form systems with phrases found separately elsewhere.

C

Ps. 105:1   הודו ליהוה קראו בשמו הודיעו בעמים עלילותיו

Is. 12:4   ואמרתם ביום ההוא הודו ליהוה קראו בשמו

הודיעו בעמים עלילתיו הזכירו כי נשגב שמו

These phrases have been listed separately in **51** and **52**. Note that the order has been changed in the second example and that they do not appear in the same line.

D

Ps. 96:13   לפני יהוה כי בא (כי בא) לשפט הארץ

ישפט תבל בצדק ועמים באמונתו

Ps. 98:9   לפני יהוה כי בא לשפט הארץ

ישפט תבל בצדק ועמים במישרים

These phrases have already been listed separately in **54** and **135**.

E

Ps. 31:2–4   בך יהוה חסיתי אל אבושה לעולם   *a*

בצדקתך פלטני הטה אלי אזנך   *b*

מהרה הצילני היה לי לצור מעוז   *c*

לבית מצודות להושיעני כי סלעי ומצודתי אתה   *d*

Ps. 71:1–3   בך יהוה חסיתי אל אבושה לעולם   *e*

בצדקתך תצילני (ותפלטני) הטה אלי אזנך   *f*

והושיעני היה לי לצור מעון   *g*

לבוא תמיד צוית להושיעני כי סלעי ומצודתי אתה   *h*

Some of these phrases have been listed separately. For *a* and *e*, see **45**. For the first parts of *b* and *f*, see **51**. For the last part of *b* and *f*, see **6**. For the last part of *d* and *h*, see **56**. The first part of *h* may be a mistake for the first part of *d*.

The amount of material in each of these examples of runs varies. In **C** two cola are repeated. In **D** two lines are repeated. In **E** a considerable block of material is repeated. Many of the phrases are not limited in their occurrence to these blocks of material.

Then, secondly, there are examples of possible runs in which most if not all of the phrases are found in no other place.

F

Ps. 29:1.2   הבו ליהוה בני אלים

הבו ליהוה כבוד ועז

הבו ליהוה כבוד שמו

השתחוו ליהוה בהדרת קדש

Ps. 96:7–9   הבו ליהוה משפחות עמים הבו ליהוה כבוד ועז

הבו ליהוה כבוד שמו שאו מנחה ובאו לחצרותיו

השתחוו ליהוה בהדרת קדש חילו מפניו כל הארץ

G

Ps. 135:10–12   שהכה גוים רבים והרג מלכים עצומים

לסיחון מלך האמרי ולעוג מלך הבשן

ולכל ממלכות כנען

ונתן ארצם נחלה נחלה לישראל עמו

Ps. 136:17–22	למכה מלכים גדלים	כי	לעולם חסדו
	ויהרג מלכים אדירים	כי	לעולם חסדו
	לסיחון מלך האמרי	כי	לעולם חסדו
	ולעוג מלך הבשן	כי	לעולם חסדו
	ונתן ארצם לנחלה	כי	לעולם חסדו
	נחלה ישלראל עבדו	כי	לעולם חסדו

Note the addition of a refrain in the second example.

H

Ps. 115:4–8   עצביהם כסף וזהב מעשה ידי אדם

פה להם ולא ידברו עינים להם ולא יראו

אזנים להם ולא ישמעו אף להם ולא יריחון

ידיהם ולא ימישון רגליהם ולא יהלכו לא יהגו בגרונם

כמוהם יהיו עשיהם כל אשר בטח בהם

Ps. 135:15–18   עצבי הגוים כסף וזהב מעשה ידי אדם

פה להם ולא ידברו עינים להם ולא יראו

אזנים להם ולא יאזינו אף אין יש רוח בפיהם

כמוהם יהיו עשיהם כל אשר בטח בהם

Note that the first example has an extra line not found in the second.

I

Ps. 115:9–11 ישראל בטח (ב)יהוה עזרם ומגנם הוא

בית אהרן בטחו (ב)יהוה עזרם ומגנם הוא

יראי יהוה בטחו (ב)יהוה עזרם ומגנם הוא

Ps. 135:19–20 בית ישראל ברכו (את) יהוה בית אהרן ברכו (את)יהוה

בית הלוי ברכו (את) יהוה יראי יהוה בלכו (את) יהוה

Note the refrain in the first example which does not appear in the second.

J

Ps. 56:14 כי הצלת נפשי ממות הלא רגלי מדחי

להתהלך לפני אלהים באור החיים

Ps. 116:8.9 כי חלצת נפשי ממות את עיני מן דעמה את רגלי מדחי

אתהלך לפני יהוה בארצות החיים

See also **44**.

K

Ps. 54:5 (כי) זרים קמו עלי ועריצים בקשו נפשי

לא שמו אלהים לנגדם

Ps. 86:14 (אלהים) זדים קמו עלי ו(עדת) עריצים בקשו נפשי

ולא שמוך לנגדם

In most of the examples **F** to **K** a considerable block of material is repeated.

One additional possibility may be cited:

L

Ps. 22:10–11 כי אתה גחי מבטן מבטיחי על שדי אמי

עליך השלכתי מרחם מבטן אמי אלי אתה

Ps. 71:5–6   כי אתה תקותי_אדני יהוה מבטחי מנעורי

עליך נסמכתי מבטן ממעי אמי אתה גוזי

See **34.**

Finally there are also a few examples in which one set of lines is found outside psalmodic literature.

M

Ps. 68:8–9   אלהים בצאתך לפני עמך בצעדך בישימון

ארץ רעשה אף שמים נטפו מפני אלהים

זה סיני מפני אלהים אלהי ישראל

Judg. 5:4   יהוה בצאתך משעיר בצעדך משדה אדום

ארץ רעשה גם שמים נטפו גם עבים נטפו מים

הרים נזלו מפני יהוה זה סיני מפני יהוה אלהי ישראל

N

Ps. 79:6–7   שפך חמתך אל הגוים אשר לא ידעוך

ועל ממלכות אשד בשמך לא קראו

כי אכל את יעקב ואת נוהו השמו

Jer. 10:25   שפך חמתך על הגוים אשר לא ידעוך

ועל משפחות אשר בשמך לא קראו

כי אכלו את יעקב ואכלהו ויכלהו ואת נוהו השמו

O

Ps. 135:7   מעלה נשאים מקצה הארץ ברקים למטר עשה

מוצא רוח מאוצרותיו

Jer. 10:13   לקול תתו המון מים בשמים ויעלה נשאים מקצה ארץ
(51:16)   ברקים למטר עשה ויוצא רוח מאצרותיו

Although the above examples fit the definition of a run, it must be conceded that they are not particularly impressive as examples of runs. The groups that do appear three times contain only two cola. The groups in which a number of lines are repeated are found only twice. Nevertheless, these groups of phrases may be cited as instances of runs, and furthermore they contain a few features that might be expected in oral style. For example, some of the phrases are not limited to these examples but are found elsewhere, suggesting that much of the language involved is widely used. Again, the repetition in the examples from **A** to **K** is never exact. There are occasional changes in the order of the cola and there are frequent instances of substitution. Sometimes words and even cola are found in one group but not in the other.

The psalms do have an adding style that is characteristic of much oral poetry. The line, composed normally of two cola, seems to be the unit of composition. In other words, the poetry has been composed by adding line to line. The end of each line is also a natural break in the syntactic structure, enjambment being rarely if ever present. This, however, is true of Hebrew poetry in general and so can hardly be used as a criterion for distinguishing orally composed poetry from literary poetry. Nevertheless, since the adding style of Hebrew poetry corresponds to the style often found in oral poetry, it is not unreasonable to suppose that Hebrew poetry may have achieved this style in an oral period. It would follow that this style became so well established in the oral period that it continued to be the normal style well into the literary period.

No clear examples of contradictions due to oral formulaic composition can be cited. This is not surprising. The examples of this phenomenon from other oral poetry mentioned earlier concerned inappropriate adjectives in noun-adjective combinations. Since this combination is not nearly as common in Hebrew as in some other languages, no stock epithets have developed in Hebrew poetry which could be used inappropriately.

The last group of characteristics mentioned were all related to the fact that formulaic language is traditional language. Although an examination of the listed phrases from this point of view does not yield a great deal, the findings should be reviewed briefly.

It was suggested that formulas with striking arrangements of consonants or vowels tend to have a long life in the tradition. The Hebrew formulas and formulaic phrases in the list do show some evidence of such arrangements. There is, for example, the combination of vowels and consonants in group **31**:

a	– ī	ʿnī	– – –yōn	ʾnī
b	– ī	ʿnī	– – –yōn	ʾnōkī
c	– ī	– –ī	– – ʿnī	ʾnī

The vowel /i/ is repeated at least three times in each phrase and the consonant /n/ at least twice. There is a play on the words 'nī/ and /ˈnī/. In *b* this play is spoiled by the change to /ˈnōkī/, but the /ō/ of this word goes with the preceding /yōn/. Another interesting example comes from group **E** listed among the possible runs:

Ps. 31:2–4 – – – – – s – – l – – š – l – – l –

– ṣ – – – l – – – – l – – – z – –

– – ṣ – l – – – l – – l-ṣ – – z

l – – s – – l – – š – – s-l – – s –

This contains a predominance of /l/ and sibilants. These two examples will be sufficient inasmuch as these features, while interesting, are not of critical importance for establishing oral style since such combinations play a role in written poetry also.

Another thing noticed about traditional formulas was that they could preserve elements from earlier times or even words or forms from foreign traditions. Elements of this sort are not more noticeable among the listed formulas and formulaic phrases than among the other language of the psalms. As far as archaic words are concerned, it is not easy to isolate them at all in such a small body of material as the biblical psalms. Unusual forms which are apt to be archaic are more easily seen.[5] There are a few archaic forms found among the listed material, e.g. **43c** contains a suffix that may be archaic,[6] and the phrase in **65** contains an old Hebrew relative pronoun. But such archaic forms do not appear in the listed phrases more than they do in the rest of psalm literature. As for foreign elements, a glance at parallel Ugaritic material which scholars have already identified shows that possible foreign words and forms are not found more frequently than elsewhere.[7]

Next, it was discovered that in a tradition of oral formulaic composition there is usually a body of formulas and formulaic patterns common to a great many poets over a long period of time. The Hebrew formulas and formulaic patterns that occur three times or more in different places testify to the fact that we are dealing with

[5] M. Tsevat lists a number of items which he holds to be psalmodic in style in *A Study of the Language of the Biblical Psalms* ("Journal of Biblical Literature Monograph Series," vol. 9 [1955]), pp. 24ff. His theory is based on the relative frequency of the occurrence of these items in the biblical psalms in comparison. The examples that follow are from his list.

[6] This is often identified as an Aramaism; for example, H. J. Kraus, *Psalmen, Biblischer Kommentar* (Neukirchen: Neukirchener Verlag, 1960), p. 116.

[7] See J. H. Patton, *Canaanite Parallels in the Book of Psalms* (Baltimore: Johns Hopkins Press, 1944) and J. Gray, *The Legacy of Canaan* ("Supplements to Vetus Testamentum," vol. 5 [1957]).

a body of common language. The body of material is likely only part of what must have been a much larger stock, just as the present psalms are probably only a small part of all the psalms originally composed.

As will be seen in the next chapter, the material can be divided roughly into two groups: phrases coming from individual complaints and phrases coming from hymns. Thus one might say that two stocks of traditional language can be discerned corresponding to two different types of poems. Even so there is a certain amount of overlapping.

Finally, it was seen that traditional formulaic language could survive considerable changes in the religion and culture of a people or a district. There are indications that among the phrases of the list we have language that has survived the change from Canaanite to Hebrew religion. For example, Yahweh is called a great king and referred to as *'elyon* in **57**. Yahweh reigns as king in **58**. Yahweh's judging the world is mentioned in **54** and **135**. These phrases are among those that some scholars claim go back ultimately to Canaanite religion.[8] This persistence is historically possible. When David took Jerusalem and established it as his capital, he may have taken over some of the Jebusite cultic traditions and adapted them for his own use. This may be the source of references of Yahweh as *'elyon*, king, the one who is lord of all the earth and the one who judges the world. It is worth noting that the groups of phrases just referred to come largely from such psalms as 9, 47, 93, 96, 97, 98, and 99, all of which have marked similarities in content.

A qualification should be added at this point. There is still a measure of uncertainty about the phrases called formulas and formulaic phrases. Oral formulaic composition may not be responsible for all of them. This is especially true of the phrases that appear only twice. Isolated instances of borrowing may have taken place, and so may account for some of the repetition. The similarity of some phrases may be mere coincidence. Other phrases may be idioms. There is no way, however, of identifying such phrases and setting them aside. All phrases conforming to the definition of the formula and the formulaic phrase had to be listed. The fact that a few phrases might be wrongly included in the evidence does not weaken the main argument since neither the whole body of phrases nor even a sizable portion of it could be explained by borrowing, coincidence, and idiomatic language.

There remains only to mention the device of theme, which will only be touched upon since the part it plays, if any, cannot be clearly

---

[8] H. J. Kraus, *Psalmen*, pp. 197ff. and the works cited there. See also Mowinckel, *The Psalms in Israel's Worship*, I, 36f.

stated. The theme was defined in terms of content and refers to elements of subject matter or a group of ideas repeated in a variable form. This was found in oral narrative poems in a larger and a smaller form. The larger form consisted of a full scene or description of some sort. The smaller form, which might be called a motif, is a smaller group of ideas or details. In oral narrative, the theme is an important device in the building of long poems. Poets use formulas and formulaic phrases to build lines, add lines together on the framework of themes, and join themes together to form poems.[9] Thus, theme is an intermediate structural device between the line and the poem itself.

Although theme was defined in terms of long, oral narrative poems, it was suggested earlier that it seemed reasonable to expect a comparable device in short poems. Might there not be larger elements beyond the formula and the line on which or around which formulas and formulaic phrases could be arranged? Such elements might be small motifs, recurrent groups of ideas or details in a variable form. Or, the framework of a particular type of poem might itself act as an outline upon which the formulas could be arranged.

Since there is no description based upon field studies of how such a device might function in short poems, it is too soon to make definite statements about the use of theme in the biblical psalms, much less to use such statements as evidence for oral composition. Nevertheless, one or two likely areas of study might be pointed out to show that there is scope for investigation along these lines.

The relative stability in the form of a type such as the individual complaint might be due to the use of this form as a device for composing psalms orally just as the theme is used in narrative poetry. Among the elements of the complaint there appears to have been no rigid rule about the way the elements may be expressed or the order in which they might appear, since there is considerable freedom and variety within a general stability among the complaints in the Old Testament. Thus, the repeated group of elements appearing in a variable form in individual complaints recalls the definition of the theme. But there are also factors that recommend caution. The cultic background of the psalms likely played a part in shaping the form of the complaint.[10] The ritual context of a complaint prayer could account for the presence of the elements. For example, a prayer

---

[9] A. B. Lord, "The Poetics of Oral Creation," in W. P. Friedrich (ed.), *Comparative Literature* ("Proceedings of the Second Congress of the International Comparative Literature Association, 1958" [Chapel Hill: University of North Carolina Press, 1959]), I, 1.

[10] See H. Gunkel and J. Begrich, *Einleitung in die Psalmen, Göttinger Handkommentar zum Alten Testament* (Göttingen: Vandenhoeck & Ruprecht, 1933), pp. 10–31; also Mowinckel, *The Psalms in Israel's Worship*, I, 25.

46124

which is a complaint would naturally have an invocation, a complaint, and a prayer for help. Furthermore, the parallel between the elements usually found in a complaint and the details normally found in a stock scene or description is not a clear one. Consequently, the extent to which the relative stability of form in some types of psalms is due to oral composition must remain for the moment undecided.

Another, and possibly more fruitful, area for thematic material might be very small units of description, perhaps better called "motifs" than "themes." An example of this would be the ways in which the enemies are often pictured in individual complaints and other psalms. They are spoken of as attackers, hunters, and wild animals, and some of these descriptions resemble one another quite noticeably, although the wording is always different. The enemy is described as one armed for the attack with a bow and arrows (Ps. 7:13) or with a sword and a bow (Ps. 37:14). The same language is used in Ps. 7:3 (of Yahweh? or an enemy?) where the attacker also has a sword and a bow. On other occasions the enemies appear as hunters who have set nets and dug pits (Ps. 7:16, 9:16, 35:7, and 57:7) into which they often fall themselves. Sometimes the enemy is a wild animal, such as a lion lying in wait to tear to pieces his prey (Ps. 7:3, 10:9, 17:13, and 57:5).

6

Distribution of the Phrases

THE PHRASES that have been identified as formulas and formulaic phrases are distributed among the psalms as might be expected of oral formulaic language. This may be shown by examining the distribution from three points of view. The first will demonstrate that the formulaic language clusters in significant amounts in a small number of psalms. The second will show that these psalms with high formulaic content come from a limited number of types of psalms. The last will indicate how phrases from these psalm types are spread fairly evenly among the elements characteristic of these types.

The first kind of distribution just mentioned is the most important for establishing oral formulaic style, since it is known that formulas and formulaic phrases are present to a high degree in individual poems composed orally by the formulaic method. An important test for oral formulaic composition is the establishing of the percentage of formulas and formulaic phrases in a given section of text.

The over-all distribution of the phrases in the biblical psalms may be seen very easily by establishing the percentage of these phrases in each psalm. This is done in the following table. For a given psalm, the total number of cola appearing in the list in the preceding chapter was placed over the total number of cola in the psalm. This fraction was then translated into a percentage. These percentages, however, are intended only as a rough guide, since for reasons already explained such figures are always relative to the total body of material available for study.

For the following table, the biblical psalms have been divided into three groups: those having a percentage of forty or over, those having a percentage of between twenty and forty, and those having a percentage under twenty. Only psalms of the first two groups have been listed. Since most of the psalms have a percentage under twenty, they do not appear in the table.

Over 40%	Between 20% and 40%

INDIVIDUAL COMPLAINTS

Ps. 6 (48%)	Ps. 27:7–14 (40%)
Ps. 40:13–18 (50%)	Ps. 28 (26%)
Ps. 54 (53%)	Ps. 31 (40%)
Ps. 86 (49%)	Ps. 35 (24%)
Ps. 142 (65%)	Ps. 61 (35%)
Ps. 143 (60%)	Ps. 71 (36%)
	Ps. 120 (21%)

INDIVIDUAL THANKSGIVINGS

Ps. 9:2–15 (42%)	Ps. 30 (29%)
	Ps. 116 (27%)
	Jon. 2:3–10 (30%)
	Possibly also Is. 12:1–6 (31%), although this is not a normal example of the type

HYMNS

Ps. 96 (65%)	Ps. 100 (33%)
Ps. 97 (42%)	Ps. 111 (27%)
Ps. 98 (50%)	

COMPLAINT OF THE PEOPLE

Ps. 79 (33%)

SPECIAL CASES

Ps. 144:1–11 (40%, including much doubtful material), which is often thought to have a close relationship with Ps. 18 (20%)
Ps. 135 (57%), which is often thought to have a close relationship with Ps. 115 (39%)

Thus the table shows that there is a definite clustering of phrases to a relatively high percentage in a small number of psalms. A total of twenty-six psalms appear in the table. Of these, eleven have a percentage over forty and fifteen have percentages between twenty and forty. In two psalms the percentage is as high as sixty-five, and five more have a percentage of fifty or over.

Three types of psalms predominate: the individual complaint, the individual thanksgiving, and the hymn. Since the complaints and thanksgivings are so closely related and have a great deal of subject matter in common, they could be considered one group as far as common language is concerned. Moreover, three of the five hymns belong to a group of psalms that are closely related in content:

Psalms 47, 93, 96, 97, 98, 99, and possibly 95.[1] One of the outstanding themes appearing in these psalms is the kingship of Yahweh. The complaints and thanksgivings, on the other hand, do not appear to have any particular themes in common which would set them apart as a special group.

In order to illustrate and explain the table, the psalms that have percentages of over forty and Psalm 144 will be treated more fully. In the first place, Hebrew texts of two of the psalms, 142 and 96, will be presented in full. Formulas and formulaic phrases will be underlined in the same way in which they were underlined when first presented above. Below each psalm, the number of the group to which each formula or formulaic phrase belongs will be given. For the remaining psalms, the Hebrew text will not be given but the formulaic material will be identified verse by verse with references to the number of the group in which the phrase appears. Finally, all the psalms will be commented upon where necessary.

PSALM 142

קולי אל יהוה אזעק קולי אל יהוה אתחנן 2

אשפך לפניו שיחי צרתי לפניו אגיד 3

(ב)התעטף עלי רוחי (ו)אתה ידעת נתיבתי 4
בארח זו אהלך טמנו פח לי

הביט ימין וראה ואין לי מכיר 5
אבד מנוס ממני אין דורש לנפשי

זעקתי אליך יהוה אמרתי אתה מחסי 6
חלקי בארץ החיים

הקשיבה אל רנתי כי דלותי מאד 7
הצילני מדדפי כי אמצו ממני

הוציאה ממסגר נפשי להודות את שמך 8
בי יכתרו צדיקים כי תגמל עלי

vs. 2:	**7**	vs. 6:	**8 ?, 33**
vs. 4:	**29, 32, 65, 25**	vs. 7:	**73, 96, 14**
vs. 5:	**112**	vs. 8:	**75, 43**

[1] H. Gunkel and J. Begrich, *Einleitung in die Psalmen, Göttinger Handkommentar zum Alten Testament* (Göttingen: Vandenhoeck & Ruprecht, 1933), pp. 95ff.; S. Mowinckel, *The Psalms in Israel's Worship*, trans. D. R. Ap-Thomas (2 vols.; Oxford: Blackwell), I, 106ff.

PSALM 96

1   שירו ליהוה שיר חדש שירו ליהוה כל הארץ

2   שירו ליהוה ברכו שמו בשרו מיום ליום ישועתו

3   ספרו (בגוים כבודו) ב(כל ה)עמים נפלאותיו

4   (כי) גדול יהוה ומהלל מאד נורא הוא על כל אלהים

5   כי כל אלהי העמים אלילים ויהוה שמים עשה

6   הוד והדר לפניו עז ותפארת במקדשו

7   הבו ליהוה משפחות עמים הבו ליהוה כבוד ועז

8   הבו ליהוה כבוד שמו שאו מנחה ובאו לחצרותיו

9   השתחוו ליהוה בהדרת קדש חילו מפניו כל הארץ

10   אמרו בגוים יהוה מלך אף תכון תבל בל תמוט
   ידין עמים במישרים

11   ישמחו השמים (ו)תגל הארץ ירעם הים ומלאו

12   יעלז שדי וכל אשר בו אז ירננו כל עצי יער

13   לפני יהוה כי בא (כי בא) לשפט הארץ
   ישפט תבל בצדק ועמים באמונתו

vs. 1:	**48, 49**		vss. 7, 8, 9:	**F**
vs. 2:	**51**		vs. 10:	**58, 133, 54**
vs. 3:	**52**		vs. 11:	**147, 127**
vs. 4:	**56, 57**		vs. 13:	**135, 54, D**

PSALM 6

vs. 2:	**81**		vs. 9:	**6**
vs. 3:	**16**		vs. 10:	**3**
vs. 5:	**109, 17, 12**		vs. 11:	**40?**
vs. 8:	**88**			

Psalm 6 is an individual complaint. There is nothing that would indicate early or late composition.

PSALM 40:13–18

vs. 13:	26	vs. 16:	94
vs. 14:	19	vs. 17:	60, 148
vs. 15:	40	vs. 18:	31, 35

Psalm 40:13–18 must have originally constituted a separate complaint of the individual. Apart from some minor variations vss. 14–18 appear again in the Psalter as Psalm 70. On the basis of content, Psalm 40 falls naturally into two parts: vss. 2–12 and vss. 13–18. The first verse of the second section, vs. 13, is not found in Psalm 70, and it is difficult to judge whether it was part of the original psalm or was added when the two parts were joined together.

It might be asked whether this psalm does not have a special relationship to Psalm 35, seeing that the two psalms have a number of phrases in common. There are three clear instances of language common to both psalms. Compare 40:15 with 35:26, 40:16 with 35:21, and 40:17 with 35:27. But these are only three of a total of eight instances, listed above, of contact with other psalms on the part of Psalm 40. Consequently, as far as Psalm 40:13–18 is concerned there is no exclusive use of material from Psalm 35. Moreover, Psalm 35 has contacts with psalms other than Psalm 40:13–18, as evidenced by groups **40, 39, 22**, and possibly **26** and **23** also, and thus has no exclusive connection with this psalm.

PSALM 54

| vs. 3: | 18 | vs. 5: | K |
| vs. 4: | 2, 73 | vs. 8: | 103, 104 |

Psalm 54 is a good example of an individual complaint. The elements usually associated with this type are present in some form: invocation and prayer (vss. 3 and 4), complaint (vs. 5), motivation (vs. 6), wish (vs. 7), vow (vs. 8), and an expression of certainty (vs. 9). There is nothing to indicate the time of composition.

PSALM 86

vs. 1:	1, 31	vs. 6:	3, 6	vs. 14:	K
vs. 2:	17	vs. 11:	13, 106	vs. 15:	55
vs. 3:	16	vs. 12:	64, 42	vs. 16:	11
vs. 4:	9	vs. 13:	44		

PSALM 142

The full text is given above.

PSALM 143

vs. 1:	2, 73, 18	vs. 8:	63, 37?, 65, 9
vs. 3:	92, 170?	vs. 9:	14
vs. 4:	29	vs. 10:	34
vs. 5:	98, 105	vs. 11:	75
vs. 7:	20, 21, 24	vs. 12:	97

Psalms 86, 142, and 143 are further examples of complaints of the individual. There are no indications of the period in which these psalms were composed.

PSALM 9:2–15

vs. 2:	64, 61	vs. 11:	150
vs. 3:	60, 41	vs. 12:	50, 52
vs. 9:	54	vs. 14:	15
vs. 10:	171?	vs. 15:	61

Psalm 9:2–15 presents a problem. Were these verses originally a separate psalm or were they always part of the one long psalm of our present Psalter, consisting of Psalms 9 and 10? There are a number of things to indicate that these two psalms were originally one: they are one in the Greek; Psalm 10 has no title; and Psalm 9 ends with the word *selah*. These facts show at least that at a very early period the two psalms were treated as one. But the strongest evidence that they were originally one is the part of an acrostic order joining the two psalms that can be made out. On the other hand, there is evidence suggesting that the two were not originally one psalm. The acrostic order is not complete and is seen clearly only in 9:2–6, 9:10–18, and 10:12–18. Furthermore, Psalm 9:2–15, including possibly vs. 16 and even a verse or two more, is a thanksgiving of the individual. The rest of Psalm 9 and all of Psalm 10 is a complaint of the individual. This combination of a thanksgiving followed by a complaint in one psalm is not common. A similar situation applies in Psalms 27 and 40, but both of these are usually taken as combinations of two psalms. Psalm 9:2–15 is almost fifty per cent formulaic language while the rest of 9 and all of 10 have almost none. It is evident that the question of the unity of Psalms 9 and 10 is not clear. Thus a proper evaluation of the presence of considerable common language in the first part and the absence of it in the second part is not possible.[2]

[2] S. Holm-Nielsen, "The Importance of Late Jewish Psalmody for the Understanding of Old Testament Psalmodic Tradition," *Studia Theologica*, XIV (1960), 50ff. It is argued in this article that Psalms 9 and 10 were originally two psalms.

PSALM 96

The full text is given above.

PSALM 97

vs. 1:	58, 147	vs. 6:	137
vs. 2:	132	vs. 8:	149
vs. 3:	67	vs. 9:	57
vs. 4:	142	vs. 12:	114, 116

PSALM 98

vs. 1:	48, 130	vs. 5:	50
vs. 3:	167	vs. 7:	127
vs. 4:	49	vs. 9:	135, 54, D

Psalms 96, 97, and 98 can be treated together. The main point requiring comment is the relationship of these three psalms to Deutero-Isaiah. Commentators are quick to draw attention to the fact that thoughts expressed in these psalms are similar to thoughts expressed by Deutero-Isaiah. Some have concluded that these psalms were written after the time of Deutero-Isaiah and show dependence on the unknown prophet. From the point of view of the phrases in the list given above, however, Psalms 96, 97, and 98 are more closely related to each other and a few other psalms than they are to Deutero-Isaiah. There are only two occurrences of phrases from Deutero-Isaiah in the list. These are in groups **48** and **167**. In **48** the phrase in question appears only once in Deutero-Isaiah but three times in the biblical psalms. This example tends to support the view that the unknown prophet borrowed from psalmodic tradition. Thus, there is only one case, **167**, that might be put forward as an example of a psalmist's borrowing from Deutero-Isaiah. Furthermore, these psalms show a high amount of language common to themselves and others. If there is any dependence, it would appear to be on the side of Deutero-Isaiah. The date of these psalms, then, cannot be assigned with any certainty to the period following Deutero-Isaiah. On the contrary, there is support for an earlier date. It was pointed out in the previous discussion of traditional stocks of common language that these psalms may contain pre-Israelite cultic material.

PSALM 144:1–11

vs. 1:	122	vs. 6:	174 ?
vs. 2:	176 ?, 66	vs. 9:	118
vs. 5:	172 ?, 141		

Psalm 144:1–11 has a surprising number of similarities with Psalm 18. The psalms involved in the seven cases in which phrases from this psalm appear among the groups in the list are as follows:

122 —	18:35, 144:1	**141** —	144:5, 104:32
176 —	18:3, 144:2, 91:2, 28:7	**174** —	18:15, 144:6
66 —	18:48, 47:4, 144:2	**118** —	144:9, 33:2
172 —	18:10, 144:5		

References to Psalm 18 appear in five of these seven groups. Only three of these involve only Psalms 18 and 144, viz., **122**, **172**, and **174**. Some further comments can be made concerning these. In **122** the phrase in Psalm 144 is at the beginning of the psalm while the phrase in Psalm 18 is at the end of the psalm. In **172** and **174** the phrases from Psalm 144 are in adjacent verses while in Psalm 18 the verses are separated by a number of lines. It should be noted further than in all these instances of exclusive connection changes have been made in the phrases. In **122** a half-line has been expanded to a full line. In **172** there has been expansion and a change of person. In **174** there is a change in the position of the words in the line. In view of all this, the possibility of the dependence of Psalm 144 on Psalm 18 is not as great as might be imagined at first glance.

PSALM 135

vs. 1:	**113**		vss. 10–12:	**G**
vs. 2:	**158**		vss. 15–18:	**H**
vs. 6:	**125**		vss. 19–20:	**I**
vs. 7:	**O**			

Psalm 135 is noteworthy in many respects. It has eight parallels with other literature, but each of these groups is the kind in which there are only two phrases, a reference to Psalm 135 and to one other. Psalm 135 is unusual in this regard, since all other psalms with rather high percentages have a good number of parallels that occur in at least two other places. Psalm 135 is also unusual in that four instances of larger blocks of material are involved; the groups listed above as **G**, **H**, **I**, and **O**. All this might imply that the author of Psalm 135 was dependent on other psalms for much of his material. The dependence, however, is not as close as might be expected. For example, in **G** the common material appears in each psalm in a different form: Psalm 136 has a refrain and Psalm 135 has an extra colon which is not found in Psalm 136. In **H**, although the wording is for the most part the same, there are differences. In **I** there is a refrain in Psalm 115 that is not found in Psalm 135. In addition, Psalm 135 has an extra line not found in Psalm 115.

The second view of distribution, consisting of an examination of the way phrases are dispersed among psalm types, has already been anticipated above, where it was seen that the psalms with the most formulaic material were mostly individual complaints or hymns. In the list of formulas and formulaic phrases, groups 1 to 47 and 73 to 106 consist mostly of phrases from individual complaints or phrases similar to those found in complaints, such as phrases from individual thanksgivings. Groups 48 to 58 and 113 to 143 are largely phrases from hymns.

Finally, the last kind of distribution may be considered. This consists in exploring how the phrases are distributed among the elements of the individual complaint and the hymn, two types in which the phrases are found to a high degree.

There are certain elements that are present in most examples of the individual complaint.[3] The mention of the divine name, usually in the opening lines of the complaint, is the invocation. Very often this invocation is accompanied by a prayer for hearing or a call for help. An important part of such a psalm is the complaint, the reason for which the prayer is offered. Closely associated with the complaint is the prayer for help, which is always in the masculine singular of the imperative. Preceding and following the expressions of complaint and prayer can often be found statements intended to influence Yahweh towards a favourable response. Such statements may be gathered under the one term "motivations." There may then be the expression of a wish in the jussive. The petitioner may also make a vow he intends to keep if the prayer is answered. Finally, there may be a statement expressing certainty that the prayer has been heard. All these elements need not be present in any one complaint psalm. The ones found most commonly are the invocation with a prayer for hearing, the complaint, the prayer, and motivations.

The phrases from the list are distributed among these elements of the complaint of the individual in the following way:

Prayer for hearing or call for help, usually with invocation: 1 to 10 and 73
   Imperative: 1 to 6 and 73 (of these, 1, 4, and 73 lack a vocative with a divine name)
   Imperfect first singular: 7 to 9
   Jussive: 10
Prayer for help: 11 to 23 and 74 to 83
   Imperative: 11 to 20 and 74 to 81
   Negative of the imperative: 21 to 23, 82 and 83
Complaints: 24 to 30 and 84 to 94

---

[3] Gunkel and Begrich, *Einleitung in die Psalmen*, pp. 172ff.; J. W. Wevers, "A Study in the Form Criticism of Individual Complaint Psalms," *Vetus Testamentum*, VI (1956), 80–96.

Motivations: **31** to **39** and **95** to **97**
  ki clauses: **31**, **34** to **38**
Wish: **40**. The forms here are either imperfect, third person plural or jussive. If they are jussive, each statement is then a wish, which in this case amounts to a curse against enemies. If they are imperfect, each is a statement of assurance that the enemies will be thwarted.
Vows or expressions of assurance of being heard: **41** and **42**, **101** to **104**

The hymns have fewer elements, only two of which are mentioned here:

Exhortations to praise: **48** to **52** and **113** to **119**
Statements of praise: **53** to **58** and **120** to **138**

7

The Theory in Broader Perspective

WHEN SEEN in a larger perspective, the results of this study of oral formulaic language in the biblical psalms, although limited in scope, do have wider implications which should not be overlooked. Certain obvious areas in which these implications may be seen come to mind immediately. This study should be seen in the context of Psalm research as a whole. There is also the contribution to the discussion of oral tradition in the Old Testament to consider. Then, the place of this investigation in the study of oral literature in general needs to be assessed.

The main trends in the study of the Psalter over the last few decades are well known. At the turn of the century the psalms were often viewed by scholars as poems created to celebrate particular historical events in the life of the Hebrew people. Thus the aim of criticism was to relate a psalm to a particular point in history in the light of which it might be interpreted. The authors of psalms were sometimes thought of as literary men with libraries at their disposal.[1] The date of composition tended to be assigned to late in the period after the Exile. In identifying different types of psalms Gunkel opened up a new approach to the psalms of the Old Testament.[2] He showed that the main types of psalms were very old and had their origin in the formal poetry of the cult. Yet Gunkel still argued that many of the present psalms were poems created by literary individuals who simply imitated the earlier cultic types. Following Gunkel, Mowinckel agrees that the main types of psalms originated in the cult.[3] He goes on to maintain, however, that most of the present psalms were

---

[1] See the comments of B. Duhm to Psalm 38 in *Die Psalmen, Kurzer Hand-Kommentar zum Alten Testament* (2nd ed. rev.; Tübingen: J. C. B. Mohr, 1922), p. 163.

[2] See H. Gunkel and J. Begrich, *Einleitung in die Psalmen, Göttinger Handkommentar zum Alten Testament* (Göttingen: Vandenhoeck & Ruprecht, 1933), pp. 1–31.

[3] See *The Psalms in Israel's Worship*, trans. D. R. Ap-Thomas (2 vols.; Oxford: Blackwell, 1962), II, 85ff.

composed specifically for use in the cult. As a consequence he tends to date psalms in the period before the Exile and thinks that the composers of the psalms must have been connected with the Temple.

The presence of oral formulaic language in the biblical psalms supports the idea that some types of psalms originated in the cult. This body of language suggests that there must have been a time when there was a living tradition of oral composition at least for complaints and hymns. In the case of some hymns with considerable formulaic content (e.g., Psalms 96, 97, and 98), the tradition could be a very early one going back to Canaanite religion. If the tradition of psalm composition was like the other oral traditions that have been studied, the bearers of the tradition were probably "professional" poets, well trained in their craft, whose function it was to compose psalms on behalf of people who desired a psalm to be offered.[4] These poets, then, would not be authors in the modern sense of the word, nor would any single performance produce an original text according to our standards. Rather, their aim would be to produce pleasing versions of the revered and respected traditional forms. Nevertheless, in doing so, the poet was more than a mouthpiece for his group, expressing the tradition held commonly by all. He was a mixture of preserver of tradition and creative artist and, if a good poet, able to work with the traditional material so that it received through him its finest and best expression.

When speaking specifically of the psalms which now form a part of the Old Testament, it is more difficult to be sure of their exact relationship to oral formulaic composition. We cannot be certain that any of the psalms having a relatively high formulaic content are oral compositions pure and simple. This stems from the difficulty of assessing the significance of formulaic material in texts since texts containing such matter may have originated in so many different ways.[5] Oral formulaic composition of psalms may have been supplanted by a form of oral composition which aimed at a fixed text. Or, the relatively free transmission of an oral formulaic tradition may have given way to a fixed form of transmission quite some time before the texts became fixed in writing. Then, too, the possibility of a "transitional" text must be kept open for the time being. In all the cases just mentioned, traditional oral formulaic language would

---

[4] See Y. M. Sokolov's description of such a poet in *Russian Folklore*, trans. C. R. Smith (New York: Macmillan, 1950), p. 214, quoted in the Appendix below; cf. Mowinckel's whole chapter on "Traditionalism and Personality in the Psalms," in *The Psalms in Israel's Worship*, II, 126ff.; also Mowinckel's theory that the psalmists were to be found among the temple singers in the same volume, p. 91, and *Psalmenstudien VI: Die Psalmdichter* ("Videnskapsselskapets Skrifter, II, Hist.-Filos. Klasse," 1924, no. 1 [Kristiania: Jacob Dybwad, 1924]).

[5] See the discussion in Chapter 3 above.

persist because it does not disappear from a poetic tradition the moment oral formulaic composition ceases to be practised. One of the real problems at this point is that little is known in detail about how traditional language operates in other kinds of oral composition and in the early stages of the change to a literary tradition. It should also be pointed out that the percentages of formulaic language ranging from forty to sixty-five obtained for some of the psalms, although impressive, are not high enough to make the assumption unavoidable that the psalms concerned are oral formulaic compositions.

On the other hand, it is equally difficult to say that the poems with over forty per cent formulaic language are not oral formulaic compositions. The difficulty lies in the fact, emphasized earlier, that the percentages are always relative and depend upon the total amount of material available for comparison. Thus it is at least possible that many psalms contain much more formulaic language than we are able to identify, and it might be that with more psalms from the biblical period available the percentages of many psalms would rise significantly. It can only be said that the psalms with high formulaic content may be oral formulaic compositions or come from a period very close to the time when oral formulaic composition was being practised. As the percentage of formulaic language found in a psalm decreases towards twenty per cent, there is less likelihood of oral formulaic composition. Such psalms would then be illustrations of how oral formulaic language persists after this method of composition is no longer flourishing.

Repeated phrases in the biblical psalms have not gone unnoticed in the past. Although no thorough study of the subject has been made, numerous commentators have remarked on the presence of similar language in different psalms and suggested reasons for its presence. There have been two main theories and they conform generally to the trends in Psalter research just mentioned. The earlier commentators, who thought of the psalmists as private poets, usually suggested that borrowing has taken place. More recent scholars, who see the strong influence of the cult in the Psalter, tend to speak of traditional language. The implications of a theory of oral formulaic language for these proposals should be considered.

Although the theory of borrowing was held mainly by older commentators, it has continued to a certain extent up to the present. B. Duhm frequently spoke of borrowing. For example, he referred to Psalm 143 as a "Blumenlese aus allen möglichen Klageliedern."[6] F. Baethgen made similar comments and said of Psalm 143: "auch Stellen aus den Psalmen hat der Dichter vielfach in sein Lied

---

[6] *Die Psalmen*, p. 469. See also his comments to Psalms 86 and 31.

verwebt."[7] Another commentator, E. Podechard, referred to "ces multiples emprunts ou imitations"[8] of Psalm 71 and he called the psalm of the Book of Jonah "une mosaïque de textes empruntés."[9] E. Kissane claimed that Psalm 86 was "largely composed of quotations and adaptations of passages from other psalms."[10] Even H. J. Kraus, one of the most recent commentators on the psalms, sometimes speaks of borrowing. He does this with reference to Psalm 86, although he rejects Duhm's much stronger description of the amount of borrowing in the psalm.[11]

The observations of these commentators imply the same general concept of borrowing. It is assumed that the authors of certain psalms quoted directly from other psalms which they had read or knew very well. This theory is reflected very well in two comments made by Duhm. He suggested that the author of Psalm 38 must have had a good library.[12] On another occasion he remarked that an author had read so many psalms that their phrases flowed automatically from his pen.[13] This theory is also illustrated by Gunkel's suggestion that Psalm 144 is an imitation of Psalm 18.[14] He offered this as a good example of how later authors consciously or even unconsciously imitated earlier works which they must have memorized or known extremely well.

The theory of borrowing raises a number of difficulties. One is the assumption apparently held by most commentators mentioned above that we are dealing with literary authors in a literary period. In other words, it seems to have been accepted without question by Duhm that the authors wrote out their psalms as they composed them and had manuscripts of well-known psalms available, which they could consult from time to time. But it is no easy matter to determine how widespread the practice of reading and writing was or the role it played at any time during the biblical period.

Furthermore, it appears that the suggestion of borrowing was not, as far as can be estimated, based on a study of the whole body of repeated phrases and their distribution in the biblical psalms. Even the commonly suggested cases of imitation and examples of dependence

---

[7] *Die Psalmen, Handkommentar zum Alten Testament* (3rd ed. rev.; Göttingen: Vandenhoeck & Ruprecht, 1904), p. 420. See also his comments to Psalm 86.

[8] *Le Psautier I: Traduction littérale et explication historique* ("Bibliothèque de la Faculté Catholique de Théologie de Lyon," vol. 3 [Lyon: Faculté Catholique, 1949]), p. 307.

[9] *Ibid.*, p. 147.

[10] *The Book of Psalms* (2 vols.; Dublin: The Richview Press, 1953), II, 76.

[11] *Psalmen, Biblischer Kommentar* (Neukirchen: Neukirchener Verlag, 1960), p. 597.

[12] *Die Psalmen*, p. 163.

[13] *Ibid.*, 1st ed., p. 125.

[14] H. Gunkel, *Die Psalmen, Göttinger Handkommentar zum Alten Testament* (4th ed.; Göttingen: Vandenhoeck & Ruprecht, 1926), p. 605.

of one psalm upon another do not prove conclusive under close examination. This was pointed out earlier when the relationship between Psalms 144 and 18, Psalms 135 and 115, and Psalms 40:13–18 and 35 was discussed. In none of these cases is the dependence so close or exclusive that it might be confidently offered as an example of borrowing. In addition to this, the nature and extent of the phenomenon of repeated phrases cast grave doubt on the theory of borrowing. The further fact that these phrases bear the characteristics of oral formulaic language leaves the theory of borrowing with very little support.

Of the scholars who have rejected a theory of borrowing in favour of a theory of traditional language, three might be mentioned. A. Weiser explains repeated phrases quite consistently by speaking of conventional language.[15] A comment made by A. R. Johnson when speaking of the similarity in phraseology between Psalms 96 and 98 illustrates this very well: "One must beware of seeing conscious dependence in a case of this kind. It may well be that we should think rather, of a common heritage of established phraseology. Cf. the repetition which so often occurs in the Akkadian epics and annals and in the Ugaritic texts as well as the similar stock phrases in, say, Homer."[16] Although he speaks of borrowing on some occasions, Kraus warns at other times that the conventional language of the cult must not be forgotten.[17]

This last suggestion concerning traditional language appears to have been based simply upon general observation without any attempt having been made to investigate the traditional language as a whole or to speculate on its nature. The fuller examination of the phrases in the preceding chapters not only has shown that these scholars were thinking along the right lines, since oral formulaic language is traditional language, but also permits us to be quite explicit about the nature of the tradition, its origin, and its background.

Concerning the larger subject of oral tradition in the Old Testament, two recent studies have sought to evaluate stylistic features of biblical poetry in the light of what is known in general about oral style. These studies are especially relevant because they discuss oral formulaic style in the Old Testament. The first is a monograph by Stanley Gevirtz[18] and the other is an article by William Whallon.[19]

---

[15] See, for example, his remarks on Psalm 135 in *Die Psalmen: Das Alte Testament Deutsch* (6th ed.; Göttingen: Vandenhoeck & Ruprecht, 1963), p. 544.

[16] *Sacral Kingship in Ancient Israel* (Cardiff: University of Wales Press, 1955), p. 90, n. 6.

[17] *Psalmen*, pp. 248, 490.

[18] *Patterns in the Early Poetry of Israel* ("Studies in Ancient Oriental Civilization," no. 32 [Chicago: University Press, 1963]).

[19] "Formulaic Poetry in the Old Testament," *Comparative Literature*, XV (1963), 1–14.

The monograph by Gevirtz, *Patterns in the Early Poetry of Israel*, contains only a brief discussion of poetic tradition by way of introduction. Most of his book is taken up with five studies of specific texts in which he attempts to use his interpretation of Hebrew poetic diction as a literary-critical tool. We are only concerned here with his introductory statements and may leave his applications aside, even though they are quite interesting.

The particular feature of Hebrew poetic diction with which Gevirtz is concerned is the traditional "fixed pair" of words. This phenomenon has been noted and discussed by a number of scholars beginning with Ginsberg in 1936.[20] According to Gevirtz and others, a traditionally fixed pair is a set of two words that appear in parallel cola with some degree of regularity in both Ugaritic and biblical poetry. For example, the pair of words "earth/dust," following the calculations of Gevirtz, appears in Ugaritic poetry ten times, always in the order "earth" in the first colon and "dust" in the second colon, and in the Old Testament thirteen times.[21] Gevirtz states that there are about sixty such pairs common to Hebrew and Ugaritic.[22]

The existence of so many fixed pairs has led to the supposition of a "traditional poetic diction common to Syro-Palestinian literatures."[23] Gevirtz states the theory of Ginsberg this way: "the poets of ancient Syria and Palestine had at their command a body of conventionally fixed pairs of words upon which they might freely draw in the construction of their literary compositions."[24] Gevirtz would add to this body of traditional fixed pairs occurring in Ugaritic and Hebrew also pairs that appear to be fixed in Hebrew but have not yet turned up in Ugaritic, because he is certain that such pairs likely belong to the same or a similar literary tradition. If this were done, a considerable body of pairs could be brought together.

Gevirtz carries this theory of traditional poetic diction one step further. When his studies were almost complete, his attention was drawn to the work of Milman Parry. Gevirtz saw from Parry's work that the use of traditional language of certain kinds was important for oral composition and went on to make the intriguing suggestion that the body of fixed pairs was a traditional diction created by oral poets as an aid in oral composition. If, according to Parry, the early Greek oral poets constructed their verses with formulas and formulaic

---

[20] For further references, see Gevirtz, *Patterns in the Early Poetry of Israel*, p. 3 and p. 8, n. 4; also R. G. Boling, " 'Synonymous' Parallelism in the Psalms," *Journal of Semitic Studies*, V (1960), 223.

[21] *Patterns in the Early Poetry of Israel*, p. 38.

[22] Boling claims "nearly a hundred" in " 'Synonymous' Parallelism in the Psalms," p. 223.

[23] Gevirtz, *Patterns in the Early Poetry of Israel*, p. 8.

[24] *Ibid.*, p. 3.

phrases, Gevirtz reasoned that Hebrew poets on their part used conventional fixed pairs which enabled them to produce parallel lines in oral composition. Although he believes that metre is involved in the use of fixed pairs, he is of the opinion that we do not know enough about Hebrew metre to say a great deal about it.

The article by Whallon may be taken in conjunction with the work of Gevirtz because it presents a very similar view. Whallon also suggests that the use of synonyms in parallel cola is a mark of oral style created by formulaic composition. He claims in the first place that "Hebrew parallelism may therefore be considered a prosodic requirement analogous to the Homeric hexameter and Anglo-Saxon alliteration."[25] Then secondly he argues that "Hebraic synonymy was a prosodic device analogous to the Homeric epithet and the Anglo-Saxon kenning."[26] In other words, because the main difficulty of the oral poet of the Greek epic was the hexameter, he resorted to formulas of suitable metrical value, the epithet being used to build these, to aid him in composition; but because the main difficulty for the Hebrew poet was producing parallel cola, metre not being too restrictive, he resorted to fixed pairs, or as Whallon calls them "synonymous formulas."

Thus both Gevirtz and Whallon suggest that the fixed pair was a device of oral composition for Hebrew poets corresponding to the formula used by poets in other traditions. The theory is undeniably an attractive one. It seems sensible for a number of reasons. This phenomenon of fixed pairs goes back very early to a time when oral composition was likely practised. Then again, fixed pairs appear to have been a convention, and conventional language plays a part in oral composition. Furthermore, it seems that the need to produce parallel cola would be one of the problems facing an oral poet of Hebrew, and one might expect that he would have a device to assist him in this.

On the other hand, there appear to be good reasons for not accepting this proposal. The main objection is that a study of the repeated phrases in the biblical psalms has turned up formulas and formulaic phrases very similar to those found in other poetic traditions. If the investigation of the preceding chapters is correct, it appears that the major device in Hebrew oral composition was the formula as in the other poetry that was examined. Nor does Hebrew poetic structure strongly suggest that oral poets would be more likely to develop fixed pairs rather than formulas and formulaic phrases as the major device for composition. The freedom permitted by Hebrew metre does not necessarily mean that formulas would not be used. There

[25] "Formulaic Poetry in the Old Testament," p. 2.
[26] *Ibid.*

is a great deal of latitude in the number of syllables in a line in Russian oral narrative poetry, and yet it appears that formulaic composition developed there in much the same way as it did elsewhere.[27] Then again, while parallelism is dominant in Hebrew poetry, it is not necessary that every line show this characteristic. In other words, there is something more fundamental to Hebrew poetry than parallelism, and this probably has to do with metre, which, although we cannot as yet say precisely how, restricts the cola within certain limits. Consequently the concern of the poet was not just to get parallel cola but to produce cola which also did not transgress the limitations of the poetic structure. Thus the precise relationship of fixed pairs to oral composition is not clear and remains to be defined more fully.

Finally, this study of oral formulaic language in the biblical psalms finds its place in the larger investigation of oral literature. Since it is not a field study, the results must always be treated with caution and be re-examined continually in the light of any new information field studies produce. Nevertheless, this study takes its place in the second rank with other textual studies and so makes its small contribution to the larger pattern that is taking shape.

[27] See the discussion of metre in Sokolov, *Russian Folklore*, pp. 310f.

Appendix : A Survey of Field-work and Textual Studies

THIS SURVEY includes all the studies consulted for the description of oral formulaic composition in the first three chapters. Although most of the important studies are discussed, the review is not exhaustive. The major areas of field-work along with related studies are outlined in the first three sections while the last section gives some indication of the areas not covered and future possibilities.

I

THE WORK OF PARRY AND LORD

Milman Parry, a scholar of the Classics, became interested in oral literature in connection with his study of Homer.[1] He became convinced that the highly traditional diction of the Homeric poems was in fact an oral style. Various aspects of this thesis were presented in a number of his writings, two of the most important being articles on the technique of oral composition in narrative poems.[2] These articles are still basic texts on the subject, even though they were written before Parry had begun his own field-work. His work up to this point was based on two things: a careful analysis of Homeric

---

[1] For descriptions of Parry's work, see the prefaces and introductions to A. B. Lord, *Serbocroatian Heroic Songs, Vol. I: Novi Pazar: English Translations* (Cambridge: Harvard University Press, 1954); *idem*, "Homer, Parry and Huso," *American Journal of Archaeology*, LII (1948), 34–44; H. Levin, "Portrait of a Homeric Scholar," *Classical Journal*, XXXII (1937), 259–66.

[2] "Studies in the Epic Technique of Oral Verse-Making. I: Homer and Homeric Style," *Harvard Studies in Classical Philology*, XLI (1930), 73–147; and "Studies in the Epic Technique of Oral Verse-Making. II: The Homeric Language as the Language of an Oral Poetry," *ibid.*, XLIII (1932), 1–50. For a complete bibliography of the writings of Parry, see the articles by Lord and Levin mentioned in the previous note.

style and a thorough study of all the available descriptions of oral poets and their work. Parry's study of Homer showed that almost all the lines in some passages appeared elsewhere in the Homeric poems, some as many as eleven times, in the same form, or a modified version of it. Parry took these phrases, which he called "formulas," to be traditional language which oral poets employed to aid them in rapid composition during a performance of a narrative poem. For it was known that oral poets do not as a rule recite traditional epic poems from memory but compose them while they sing or recite before an audience. Because the traditional language was so extensive in Homer, Parry estimated that it must have been the creation of generations of poets working within a tradition.[3]

During his work on Homer, Parry became dissatisfied with the information on oral poets available at that time and so he decided to undertake field studies of his own. He wished to know more about how oral poets composed their narratives. Thus in the summer of 1933 he set out for Yugoslavia to study the oral narrative poetry which still flourished there among the Southslavic peoples. Parry explained his intention this way: "In other words the study of the Southslavic poetry was meant to provide me an exact knowledge of the characteristics of oral style, in the hope that when such characteristics were known exactly their presence or absence could definitely be ascertained in other poetries, and those many large and small ways in which the one oral poetry differed from written poetry for its understanding could be carried over to the Homeric poems."[4] In other words, he wanted to observe at close quarters how an oral poet put the words, phrases, lines, passages, and themes of his poems together and what happened as poems were passed on from one singer to another and from one generation to the next. A second trip to Yugoslavia in the following year resulted in the collection of a great mass of material, not only narrative poems but also other kinds of oral literature. On the second trip Parry was accompanied by A. B. Lord.

There remained the colossal task of publishing the material collected and producing a description of the nature and characteristics of oral poetry, which was the ultimate aim of the field expeditions. Parry was killed in an accident in 1935 and the work fell to his student, Lord. Although there is still a great deal to be done, Lord has published some articles, a few of the texts, and a book on oral narrative poetry so that a great deal of information based on Parry's expeditions is

---

[3] See the introductory pages to an unfinished book by Parry on Southslavic heroic songs in Lord, *Serbocroatian Heroic Songs*, vol. I, p. 3.
    [4] *Ibid.*, p. 4.

available.[5] In addition to this, Lord made three further trips to Yugoslavia in 1937, 1950, and 1951 in order to gather more material.

The methods used by Parry and Lord in collecting material are worth mentioning because of the great care taken to ensure accurate results, the sort upon which a sound description of oral style could be constructed.[6] Material was recorded by both dictation and recording apparatus. Great care was taken in the selection of the singers from whom the songs were recorded. Furthermore, each singer was interviewed at length on a wide variety of subjects, such as his early training, his repertoire, his teachers, and his ability to read and write. The interview, which was carried out by a trained native assistant, was recorded along with the songs. The interviews were intended to show to what extent the singers were aware of the nature of the process of oral composition in which they were engaged. Sometimes Parry recorded versions of the same song from several singers, occasionally even having the same singer repeat a song, so that there might be concrete evidence of what happens to a poem when it is repeatedly performed by the same singer.

The field-work of Parry and Lord produced a number of significant results.[7] Although many facts about oral composition were known previously in a general way and others to some extent anticipated in Parry's work on Homer, statements could now be made on the basis of carefully collected evidence and could be amply supported by a wealth of concrete illustrations. In the first place, it was seen clearly that the long narrative poems of the Serbocroatians were not sung from a memorized text since each performance was different. The poets composed their songs anew during each performance with the aid of traditional language, stock scenes, and typical descriptions. The main devices aiding composition were the formula, the formulaic phrase, and the theme, all of which have been fully described above. In Lord's words, the process "consists of the building of metrical lines and half lines by means of formulas and formulaic expressions and of the building of songs by the use of themes."[8] This process is well illustrated by an experiment performed by Parry. Parry once asked an especially talented singer to listen to a song, which he had never heard before, as it was performed by another singer. Parry then asked the first singer if he could repeat this song, consisting of several thousand lines, which he had just heard for the first time.

[5] Thus far the first two volumes of *Serbocroatian Heroic Songs*, containing texts and translations of oral narrative poems and interviews with singers, have appeared. The book referred to is *The Singer of Tales* ("Harvard Studies in Comparative Literature," no. 24 [Cambridge: Harvard University Press, 1954]).

[6] For what follows, see *Serbocroatian Heroic Songs*, vol. I, pp. 6–15.

[7] For what follows, see the relevant chapters in Part I of Lord, *Singer of Tales*.

[8] *Ibid.*, p. 4.

This singer was such a master of the traditional devices of composition that he not only sang the song but produced a superior version.[9]

One final illustration may be cited to indicate the great value of the work of Parry and Lord for the understanding of the oral composition of narrative poems. One Serbocroatian poet made the claim: "If I were to live for twenty years, I would sing the song which I sang for you here today just the same twenty years from now, word for word."[10] Not twenty but seventeen years later Lord did record the same song from the same singer. A comparison of the earlier and later versions of the song showed that they were not identical. This incident demonstrates not only that songs differ from performance to performance but also that singers are not aware of this variation, or at least do not consider it significant.

OTHER STUDIES BASED ON THE WORK OF PARRY AND LORD

The impact of Parry's work on Homer is still being felt in this field, and his views have been accepted in whole or in part by a number of Homeric scholars.[11] Lord himself has emphatically supported Parry's views on Homer.[12] Another scholar who might be mentioned in this regard is J. A. Notopoulos, who has written a number of articles on the subject of oral composition and Homer.[13] One of the main points of disagreement among scholars who are favourable to Parry's views is whether or not the Homeric poems are actually oral compositions. On the one hand, Lord maintains that they are "oral dictated" texts.[14] On the other hand, Bowra claims that they are "transitional texts," that is, written by a literate poet who was trained in oral technique.[15]

The work of Parry and Lord has had its effect in the field of Old English as well, and some scholars have begun to analyse poems for evidence of oral style. The leader in this field has been F. P.

---

[9] Ibid., p. 78; see also Serbocroatian Heroic Songs, vol. I, pp. 240f., 266.

[10] Serbocroatian Heroic Songs, vol. I, p. 241.

[11] C. M. Bowra, Heroic Poetry (London: Macmillan, 1952), pp. 233–36. See the surveys of the reception of Parry's work by Homeric scholars in C. H. Whitman, Homer and the Heroic Tradition (Cambridge: Harvard University Press, 1958), pp. 1ff., and also Chapters 4 and 6; F. M. Combellack, "Milman Parry and Homeric Artistry," Comparative Literature, XI (1959), 193–208; G. P. Goold, "Homer and the Alphabet," Transactions and Proceedings of the American Philological Association, XCI (1960), 272–91.

[12] Singer of Tales, pp. 141ff.

[13] See, for example, "Continuity and Interconnexion in Homeric Oral Composition," Transactions and Proceedings of the American Philological Association, LXXXII (1951), 81–101.

[14] Singer of Tales, pp. 148ff.

[15] Heroic Poetry, pp. 233ff.

Magoun, Jr., who has discussed the use of formula and theme in Anglo-Saxon poetry, and there are other scholars who have followed his lead.[16] The diction of *Beowulf* has been examined by R. Creed, who claims the presence of four hundred different whole-verse formulas, some of which are repeated as often as twelve times.[17] These formulas make up 1200 of a total of 6394 verses in the poem, and Creed claims that there is a great deal more formulaic material beyond this. Furthermore, four poems by Cynewulf, consisting of 5194 verses, have been analysed by R. Diamond. He maintains that 2224 verses (42.8 per cent) of the poems can be established as formulaic, using only the material in these four poems for comparison.[18]

Two further significant points should be noted about the discussion of formulaic style in the field of Old English. In the first place, scholars are in general not inclined to insist that texts containing oral characteristics are oral compositions. They suggest that the works may have been composed by a lettered poet who was trained in the oral technique and who carried this technique over into his literary style.[19] Then, secondly, some critics have begun to explore the implications of oral composition for textual criticism[20] and stylistics,[21] thus opening up new and interesting possibilities for study.

Oral style has even been discussed in connection with Middle English poetry. R. A. Waldron suggests that formulas are to be found in some alliterative poetry of the fourteenth century.[22] He makes it quite clear, however, that he is not arguing that these texts were composed orally but only that the characteristics of oral style that

[16] Magoun, "Oral-Formulaic Character of Anglo-Saxon Narrative Poetry," *Speculum*, XXVIII (1953), 446–67; *idem*, "The Theme of the Beasts of Battle in Anglo-Saxon Poetry," *Neuphilologische Mitteilungen*, LVI (1955), 81–89; see also S. Greenfield, "The Formulaic Expression of the Theme of the 'Exile' in Anglo-Saxon Poetry," *Speculum*, XXX (1955), 200–6; A. Bonjour, "*Beowulf* and the Beasts of Battle," *Publications of the Modern Language Association*, LXXII (1957), 563–73; R. Creed, "The Making of an Anglo-Saxon Poem," *ELH*, XXVI (1959), 445–54; J. Campbell, "Oral Poetry in *The Seafarer*," *Speculum*, XXXV (1960), 87–96; W. A. O'Neil, "Another Look at Oral Poetry in *The Seafarer*," *Speculum*, XXXV (1960), 596–600; R. Diamond, "Theme as Ornamentation in Anglo-Saxon Poetry," *Publications of the Modern Language Association*, LXXVI (1961), 461–68; R. Creed, "The Singer Looks at His Sources," *Comparative Literature*, XIV (1962), 44–52.
[17] "On the Possibility of Criticizing Old English Poetry," *Texas Studies in Literature and Language*, III (1961), 97.
[18] "The Diction of the Signed Poems of Cynewulf," *Philological Quarterly*, XXXVIII (1959), 234.
[19] Creed, "Old English Poetry," p. 97; Diamond, "Signed Poems of Cynewulf," p. 229.
[20] R. Creed, "Genesis 1316," *Modern Language Notes*, LXXIII (1958), 321–25; Magoun, "Oral Formulaic Character . . .," pp. 458f.
[21] J. B. Bessinger, "*Beowulf* and the Harp at Sutton Hoo," *University of Toronto Quarterly*, XXVII (1957–58), 148–68; *idem*, "*Maldon* and the Óláfsdrápa: An Historical Caveat," *Comparative Literature*, XIV (1962), 23–35.
[22] "Oral-Formulaic Technique and Middle English Alliterative Poetry," *Speculum*, XXXII (1957), 792–804.

are to be seen in these poems are "the *remains* of an oral technique embedded in written literature."[23]

The last area to be mentioned in which the work of Parry and Lord has prompted discussion is the field of mediaeval French narrative poetry. The *chansons de geste* have been considered from the point of view of their use of formulas and themes by J. Rychner.[24] Recently, S. G. Nichols, Jr. has investigated the diction of the *Chanson de Roland* and come to the conclusion that oral characteristics are clearly present.[25] As in the case of the Old and Middle English scholars mentioned above, Nichols does not claim that the poem is a dictated text but that it was likely written by someone trained in the oral technique.[26]

The possibilities are not exhausted. Oral composition has also been mentioned briefly in connection with a number of other narrative traditions. In his book, *Heroic Poetry*, C. M. Bowra has discussed the role of improvisation not only in Homer, Anglo-Saxon poems, and the *Chanson de Roland* but also in the *Elder Edda* and the Spanish epic *Cid*.[27] Lord has tentatively suggested that the various manuscripts of the mediaeval Greek epic *Digenis Akritas* contain enough traces of oral style to show that an oral tradition lies behind them.[28] Finally, Notopoulos and A. Hoekstra have examined oral style in the works of Hesiod.[29]

Up to this point the poems considered have been narrative poems of considerable length, but shorter poems of different kinds have not been omitted from discussion of oral formulaic composition begun by Parry and Lord. Parry did in fact record a great many examples of other kinds of oral literature, but only a few short poems have been published to date.[30] Unfortunately, no information whatsoever has been provided about their composition or transmission. In his earlier articles on Homer, however, Parry pointed out the possibility of oral composition being practised in the Greek elegiac and lyric traditions, although he did not analyse any of the poems of these types for formulas.[31]

---

[23] *Ibid.*, p. 794.

[24] "La chanson de geste, épopée vivante," *La Table Ronde*, CXXXII (1958), 152–67.

[25] *Formulaic Diction and Thematic Composition in the Chanson de Roland* ("University of North Carolina Studies in the Romance Languages and Literatures," no. 36 [Chapel Hill: University of North Carolina Press, 1961]); Lord also discusses the *Chanson de Roland* in *Singer of Tales*, pp. 202–6.

[26] *Formulaic Diction*, p. 9, n. 2.

[27] Pp. 216ff.

[28] *Singer of Tales*, pp. 207–21.

[29] J. A. Notopoulos, "Homer, Hesiod and the Achaean Heritage of Oral Poetry," *Hesperia*, XXIX (1960), 177–97; A. Hoekstra, "Hésiode et la tradition orale," *Mnemosyne*, X (1957), 193–225.

[30] B. Bartók and A. B. Lord, *Serbo-Croatian Folk Songs* ("Columbia University Studies in Musicology," no. 7 [New York: Columbia University Press, 1951]).

[31] "Studies I," p. 92; "Studies II," p. 29.

Formulaic analysis of classical Greek poetry has been extended beyond the oral narrative, mainly by Notopoulos.[32] On the one hand, he has begun an investigation of the incidence of formulas in early lyric and elegy and claims rather high percentages of formulaic material in a few sample cases.[33] On the other hand, he has analysed four Homeric hymns and maintains that over eighty per cent of the lines in each of these hymns contains formulaic material.[34]

One very short poem in Old English, the *Hymn* of Caedmon, has been subjected to formulaic analysis by Magoun. One of his comments in this connection is worth noting. He asserts that "Caedmon might theoretically have composed his *Hymn* word by word as we compose poetry, but an analysis of the language makes abundantly clear that the *Hymn* is made up entirely of formulas or systems of formulas, in a word, that its language is quite traditional."[35] In other words, it is quite possible that this very short poem was composed orally.

Texts of Gaelic songs which have been collected in recent years in the Western Isles of Scotland have been studied from the point of view of oral style by J. Ross.[36] The informants from whom these songs were collected were not themselves practising oral composition, but it is argued that the poetry may come from an earlier tradition in which oral formulaic composition flourished. These poems vary in length from a dozen to a hundred lines and contain, according to Ross, formulas as defined by Parry and Lord. Ross, however, goes on to suggest that Parry's definition should be expanded to include "conceptual formulas," i.e., ideas that recur in different wording and different metrical form. This proposal has already been fully discussed above in connection with the devices of oral composition.

Finally, an exchange of views in the field of the ballad might be mentioned briefly. Working from the conclusions of Parry and Lord, J. H. Jones argues that the commonplace of the ballad tradition was a compositional device used by oral poets.[37] He explains that "the commonplaces, once mastered by a singer, freed him from the restriction of memorization and enabled him to compose rather than

[32] "The Homeric Hymns as Oral Poetry: A Study of Post Homeric Oral Tradition," *American Journal of Philology*, LXXXIII (1962), 337–68; *idem*, "Homer, Hesiod and the Achaean Heritage"; *idem*, "Studies in Early Greek Poetry," *Harvard Studies in Classical Philology*, LXVIII (1964), 1–77; and also, W. E. McLeod, "Oral Bards at Delphi," *Transactions and Proceedings of the American Philological Association*, XCII (1961), 317–25.

[33] "Homer, Hesiod and the Achaean Heritage," p. 181.

[34] "Homeric Hymns as Oral Poetry," pp. 358ff.

[35] "Bede's Story of Caedmon: The Case History of an Anglo-Saxon Oral Singer," *Speculum*, XXX (1955), 53.

[36] "Formulaic Composition in Gaelic Oral Literature," *Modern Philology*, LVII (1959), 1–12.

[37] "Commonplace and Memorization in the Oral Tradition of the English and Scottish Popular Ballads," *Journal of American Folklore*, LXXIV (1961), 97–112.

merely transmit."[38] In the same issue of the *Journal of American Folklore* in which the article by Jones appeared, a brief rebuttal was made by A. B. Friedman.[39] He denies that the conclusions of Parry and Lord are applicable to the ballad tradition and holds that the transmission of ballads was accomplished by memorization rather than improvisation. In other words, the matter is far from settled and only further study in this area will produce a clear answer to the problem.

II

Another report of field-work that ought to be considered is the description by M. B. Emeneau of the oral poets among the Todas, a small community of buffalo herders in south India.[40] He began his work among these people in 1935 and continued with some interruptions for three years. Emeneau is familiar with the work of Parry and so writes with an awareness of the characteristics of oral composition described in his writings and those of others associated with him. Although the songs Emeneau took down by dictation have not yet been published, his articles afford a useful summary of his findings. The songs of the Todas included those for use at funerals, weddings, and dairy ceremonials. Laments and love songs were also sung.

The poetic structure of the two hundred and fifty songs recorded by Emeneau is rather unusual.[41] Each metrical unit contains three syllables and might consist of as many as three words. A sentence in turn is composed of one to seven units. A basic principle of the poetic structure is parallelism so that each sentence must be paired with another sentence having the same syntactic structure and the same number of units. The sentences that may be brought together in this way to form couplets are largely fixed by tradition.

The poets who created songs in this unusual poetic structure employed the same technique of oral composition used by the Serbocroatian singers studied by Parry and Lord. The same general characteristics were observed by Emeneau. No two performances of a song, even by the same singer, were ever identical. This held true for old, traditional songs as well as for new songs. Furthermore,

[38] *Ibid.*, p. 103.

[39] "The Formulaic Improvisation Theory of Ballad Tradition—A Counterstatement," *Journal of American Folklore*, LXXIV (1961), pp. 113–15. See also with reference to the Spanish ballad tradition, B. A. Beatie, "Oral-Traditional Composition in the Spanish *Romancero* of the Sixteenth Century," *Journal of the Folklore Institute*, I (1964), 92–113.

[40] "The Songs of the Todas," *Proceedings of the American Philosophical Society*, LXXVII (1937), 543–60; "Oral Poets of South India—The Todas," *Journal of American Folklore*, LXXI (1958), 312–24.

[41] "Oral Poets of South India," p. 317.

a great deal of fixed phraseology was used. Emeneau points out that almost every phrase in the poetry can be found repeated at least once. It is also assumed that a long period was required to develop the highly traditional body of poetic language of the Todas, since almost every subject on which they composed songs had set patterns and phrases that could be used in composition.

It is also significant that the making of songs among the Todas was not limited to the "professional" singer. Everyone could compose songs in the traditional way. Emeneau gained the impression, however, that the best singers were usually called upon to accompany the dancers on special occasions.

III

Investigations of Russian oral literature were begun around the middle of the last century, and over the past hundred years a great deal of oral literature of various kinds has been collected.[42] Although much of the recording of this material was done with great care, neither the singers nor their songs have been examined with the same degree of thoroughness that one finds in the studies of Parry and Lord. Nor are the discussions of the traditional devices of composition as detailed as might be desired. Since these descriptions of the oral poet at work and of the poetry he produces were made quite apart from the investigations of Parry and Lord, they represent a useful independent study for comparing views.

The first important collection of this oral poetry was made by P. N. Rybnikov in the years 1859 and 1860 among the peasants of Olonets on Lake Onega.[43] In 1871, A. Gilferding visited the same area and interviewed many of the same singers heard by Rybnikov and obtained versions of many of the same songs he had collected. Much later, in the years from 1926 to 1928, the Sokolov brothers visited the same area and collected further material. Thus, versions of the same songs collected at different periods provide scholars with invaluable material for the study of oral narrative tradition spanning three, and in some cases four, generations of narrators.[44]

Collections of Russian oral literature contain both narrative and

[42] The main works to be referred to are Y. M. Sokolov, *Russian Folklore*, trans. C. R. Smith (New York: Macmillan, 1950); N. K. Chadwick, *Russian Heroic Poetry* (Cambridge: University Press, 1932); H. M. and N. K. Chadwick, *The Growth of Literature* (3 vols.; Cambridge: University Press, 1932–40), vol. II; C. M. Bowra, *Heroic Poetry*. These works contain bibliographies of earlier basic works, the most important of which are not available in English.

[43] See H. M. and N. K. Chadwick, *Growth of Literature*, II, 7ff., for a full account of what follows.

[44] Bowra discusses two such families of narrators in *Heroic Poetry*, pp. 443ff.

ceremonial poetry. The narrative poems vary considerably in length. Some songs extend to several hundred lines, while others have less than a hundred.[45] These narratives recount many of the important events and persons from the past thousand years of Russian history. An interesting group within this historical poetry is the elegy, of which there are two types: laments for famous rulers purportedly composed by their widows and laments of the troops on the death of their sovereign.[46] The ceremonial poetry consists largely of the chants used at ordinary weddings and the laments sung at funerals of the common people.

From the descriptions of the composition and transmission of Russian oral poetry given by collectors mentioned above, it is evident that we are faced with the same sort of process examined by Parry and Lord in Yugoslavia and by Emeneau in India. Poems were created anew during each performance with the use of traditional language and stock scenes and descriptions. This is apparent in a comment made by Gilferding: "each time that the *skazitel'* sings the *bylina*, he composes it there and then, sometimes adding, at other times eliminating, and sometimes changing the order of the verses or the expressions themselves."[47] Sokolov claims that the singer or chanter of oral poetry is not just a performer but also "to a considerable degree, their creator and author."[48] This parallels the view of Lord to a very significant extent.[49]

The traditional devices used in the composition of Russian oral poems have not been submitted to the thorough analysis found in the writings of Parry, Lord, and others influenced by them. Nevertheless, the comments of students of Russian oral poetry indicate the use of devices very similar to the formula and theme as they were described by Parry and Lord. Russian scholars speak of traditional, fixed language such as "static adjectives" and "static phrases."[50] These appear to be different kinds of formulas. Russian investigators also speak of "traditional formulas" but they mean by this stock scenes and descriptions rather than fixed phrases.[51] These seem to be the devices described earlier as themes.

---

[45] *Ibid.*, p. 330.

[46] H. M. and N. K. Chadwick, *Growth of Literature*, II, 62 and 159ff.

[47] Quoted in S. Skendi, *Albanian and South Slavic Oral Epic Poetry* ("Memoirs of, the American Folklore Society," vol. 44 [Philadelphia: American Folklore Society, 1954]), p. 25. See also the comments of Gilferding quoted in N. K. Chadwick, *Russian Heroic Poetry*, p. 14; and the important discussion in Sokolov, *Russian Folklore*, pp. 12f.

[48] *Russian Folklore*, p. 9.

[49] See Lord, *Singer of Tales*, pp. 4ff.

[50] H. M. and N. K. Chadwick, *Growth of Literature*, II, 71ff. and 246; also Sokolov *Russian Folklore*, pp. 302ff.

[51] Sokolov, *Russian Folklore*, pp. 305ff.

The composition of narrative and ceremonial poetry was not limited to the specialist, although, as might be expected, the best poets were those with the most talent and experience.[52] For example, in times of mourning, almost every woman was able to compose a lament in the traditional way, but often a professional mourner was called in to perform this task. Sokolov gives an interesting picture of such a professional poet:

Keeping in mind some kind of traditional plan of composition, possessing a rich store of stylistic *loci communes* (invocations, descriptive scenes), the talented weeper, having a retentive memory, with the aid of these poetic means, of this hereditary poetic stock in trade, can compose lamentations which are sometimes striking in their power, psychological fullness, and vast emotional infectiousness, and which are directly linked with the precise event in the peasant family on account of which the weeper has been summoned.[53]

One final point about Russian oral poetry should be mentioned. The structure of the line has a certain amount of flexibility as far as the number of syllables are concerned. While in Serbocroatian narrative poetry the line is strictly limited to ten syllables, the line may have as few as eight and as many as fifteen or sixteen syllables in Russian oral narrative.[54] This recalls the freedom apparent in Hebrew poetry and shows that traditional elements are still used even where flexibility in the length of the line exists.

IV

The studies mentioned above do not exhaust our information on oral composition, although what remains is sketchy and incomplete. Much of this information, most of which is to be found in the survey of the Chadwicks, contains clues that point in the direction of oral formulaic composition. For example, in speaking of extempore composition among the Tuareg of the central Sahara, the Chadwicks comment that "this facility in composition, and the constant habit of extemporizing have been aided by, and in their turn tend to perpetuate, a highly stereotyped form of diction, a conservative turn of expression, a static phraseology."[55] Another important study to which the Chadwicks refer is the work of V. V. Radlov, who collected examples of oral literature from the Tartar peoples of central Asia. His descriptions of how the Tartar poets created their poetry shows

[52] H. M. and N. K. Chadwick, *Growth of Literature*, II, 286.
[53] *Russian Folklore*, p. 214.
[54] *Ibid.*, pp. 310f.
[55] *Growth of Literature*, III, 669.

clearly that they employed the same method of composition used by the Serbocroatian poets studied by Parry and Lord.[56]

There is also the possibility of enlarging our knowledge of oral literature by further study. This is especially true with regard to the steadily dwindling number of oral cultures existing in different parts of the world. One of the scholars already referred to in another connection has recently gone into the field and studied just such an oral tradition. This investigator, Notopoulos, carried out his recording in Crete.[57] There are also textual studies that could be done. Since there are a number of texts that have come from oral cultures, these form likely subjects for analysis in order to establish oral characteristics. One possibility has been pointed out by Emeneau. He draws attention to the large number of repeated phrases in the Vedas with the suggestion that this is related to the fact that they are oral compositions.[58] Another possibility, although perhaps very limited, may be a group of songs from Ancient Egypt in which stock phrases have been found.[59]

[56] *Ibid.*, pp. 179ff. See also T. G. Winner, *The Oral Art and Literature of the Kazakhs of Russian Central Asia* (Durham: Duke University Press, 1958).

[57] See "Homeric Hymns as Oral Poetry," pp. 338f., for brief comments and references to other literature.

[58] "Oral Poets of South India," p. 313. Emeneau claims that the marks of oral composition are also present in Sanskrit epic poetry. His view is that the transmission of this poetry reflects the fact that no two recitations of the poem were exactly the same. See R. K. Sharma, *Elements of Poetry in the Mahābhārata* ("University of California Publications in Classical Philology," vol. 20 [Berkeley: University of California Press, 1964]), pp. 167–75.

[59] E. F. Wente, "Egyptian 'Make Merry' Songs Reconsidered," *Journal of Near Eastern Studies*, XXI (1962), 128.

Bibliography

ALBRIGHT, W. F. *From the Stone Age to Christianity.* 2nd ed.; New York: Doubleday, 1957.
——— "Some Oriental Glosses on the Homeric Problem," *American Journal of Archaeology,* LIV (1950), 162–76.
ALT, A. *Der Gott der Väter.* ("Beiträge zur Wissenschaft vom Alten und Neuen Testament," III. Folge, Heft 12.) Stuttgart: W. Kohlhammer, 1929.
AUSTERLITZ, R. "Ob-Ugric Metrics," *FF Communications,* 174 (1958).
BAETHGEN, F. *Die Psalmen. Handkommentar zum Alten Testament.* 3rd ed. rev.; Göttingen: Vandenhoeck & Ruprecht, 1904.
BARTÓK, B. and A. B. LORD. *Serbo-Croatian Folk Songs.* ("Columbia University Studies in Musicology," no. 7.) New York: Columbia University Press, 1951.
BEATIE, B. A. "Oral-Traditional Composition in the Spanish *Romancero* of the Sixteenth Century," *Journal of the Folklore Institute,* I (1964), 92–113.
BESSINGER, J. B. "*Beowulf* and the Harp at Sutton Hoo," *University of Toronto Quarterly,* XXVII (1957–58), 148–68.
——— "*Maldon* and the Óláfsdrápa: An Historical Caveat," *Comparative Literature,* XIV (1962), 23–35.
BLENKINSOPP, J. "Structure and Style in Judges 13–16," *Journal of Biblical Literature,* LXXXII (1963), 65–76.
BOLING, R. G. " 'Synonymous' Parallelism in the Psalms," *Journal of Semitic Studies,* V (1960), 221–55.
BONJOUR, A. "*Beowulf* and the Beasts of Battle," *Publications of the Modern Language Association,* LXXII (1957), 563–73.
BOWRA, C. M. *Heroic Poetry.* London: Macmillan, 1952.
——— "Style," in A. J. B. WACE and F. H. STUBBINGS (eds.), *A Companion to Homer.* London: Macmillan, 1962, pp. 26–37.
CAMPBELL, J. "Oral Poetry in *The Seafarer,*" *Speculum,* XXXV (1960), 87–96.
CHADWICK, H. M. and N. K. CHADWICK. *The Growth of Literature.* 3 vols.; Cambridge: University Press, 1932–40.
CHADWICK, N. K. *Russian Heroic Poetry.* Cambridge: University Press, 1932.
CHAYTOR, H. J. "Reading and Writing," *Explorations,* III (1954), 6–17.

COMBELLACK, F. M. "Milman Parry and Homeric Artistry," *Comparative Literature*, XI (1959), 193–208.

CREED, R. "Genesis 1316," *Modern Language Notes*, LXXIII (1958), 321–25.

——— "The Making of an Anglo-Saxon Poem," *ELH*, XXVI (1959), 445–54.

——— "On the Possibility of Criticizing Old English Poetry," *Texas Studies in Literature and Language*, III (1961), 97–106.

——— "The Singer Looks at His Sources," *Comparative Literature*, XIV (1962), 44–52.

CULLEY, R. C. "An Approach to the Problem of Oral Tradition," *Vetus Testamentum*, XIII (1963), 113–25.

DIAMOND, R. "The Diction of the Signed Poems of Cynewulf," *Philological Quarterly*, XXXVIII (1959), 228–41.

——— "Theme as Ornamentation in Anglo-Saxon Poetry," *Publications of the Modern Language Association*, LXXVI (1961), 461–68.

DOW, STERLING. "Minoan Writing," *American Journal of Archaeology*, LVIII (1954), 77–129.

DUHM, B. *Die Psalmen. Kurzer Hand-Kommentar zum Alten Testament.* 2nd ed. rev.; Tübingen: J. C. B. Mohr, 1922.

EISSFELDT, O. *Einleitung in das Alte Testament.* 3rd ed. rev.; Tübingen: J. C. B. Mohr, 1964.

EMENEAU, M. B. "Oral Poets of South India—The Todas," *Journal of American Folklore*, LXXI (1958), 312–24.

——— "The Songs of the Todas," *Proceedings of the American Philosophical Society*, LXXVII (1937), 543–60.

FRIEDMAN, A. B. "The Formulaic Improvisation Theory of Ballad Tradition —A Counterstatement," *Journal of American Folklore*, LXXIV (1961), 113–15.

GERHARDSSON, B. *Memory and Manuscript.* ("Acta Seminarii Neotestamentici Upsaliensis," no. 22.) Uppsala: Almqvist & Wiksells, 1961.

GEVIRTZ, S. *Patterns in the Early Poetry of Israel.* ("Studies in Ancient Oriental Civilization," no. 32.) Chicago: University Press, 1963.

GOOLD, G. P. "Homer and the Alphabet," *Transactions and Proceedings of the American Philological Association*, XCI (1960), 272–91.

GRAY, J. *The Legacy of Canaan.* ("Supplements to Vetus Testamentum," vol. 5 [1957].)

GREENFIELD, S. "The Formulaic Expression of the Theme of the 'Exile' in Anglo-Saxon Poetry," *Speculum*, XXX (1955), 200–6.

GUNKEL, H. *Die Psalmen. Göttinger Handkommentar zum Alten Testament.* 4th ed.; Göttingen: Vandenhoeck & Ruprecht, 1926.

GUNKEL, H. and J. BEGRICH. *Einleitung in die Psalmen. Göttinger Handkommentar zum Alten Testament.* Göttingen: Vandenhoeck & Ruprecht, 1933.

HARTMANN, K. "Die Rhapsodin M. S. Krjukova, ihre sowjetischen Volkspoeme und deren Verhältnis zur Tradition des grossrussischen Heldenliedes," *Die Welt der Slaven*, II (1957), 394–418.

HOEKSTRA, A. "Hésiode et la tradition orale," *Mnemosyne*, X (1957), 193–225.

HOLM-NIELSON, S. "The Importance of Late Jewish Psalmody for the

Understanding of Old Testament Psalmodic Tradition," *Studia Theologica*, XIV (1960), 1–53.

JOHNSON, A. R. *Sacral Kingship in Ancient Israel*. Cardiff: University of Wales Press, 1955.

JONES, J. H. "Commonplace and Memorization in the Oral Tradition of the English and Scottish Popular Ballads," *Journal of American Folklore*, LXXIV (1961), 97–112.

KISSANE, E. *The Book of Psalms*. 2 vols.; Dublin: Richview Press, 1953–54.

KRAUS, H. J. *Psalmen. Biblischer Kommentar*. Neukirchen: Neukirchener Verlag, 1960.

LEVIN, H. "Portrait of a Homeric Scholar," *Classical Journal*, XXXII (1937), pp. 259–66.

LITTMANN, E. "Abessinische und semitische Poesie," *Zeitschrift der Deutschen Morgenländischen Gesellschaft*, IX (1930), 207–25.

LOHR, C. H. "Oral Techniques in the Gospel of Matthew," *Catholic Biblical Quarterly*, XXIII (1961), 403–35.

LORD, A. B. "Composition by Theme in Homer and Southslavic Epos," *Transactions and Proceedings of the American Philological Association*, LXXXII (1951), 71–80.

———— "Homer, Parry and Huso," *American Journal of Archaeology*, LII (1948), 34–44.

———— "Homer and Other Epic Poetry," in A. J. B. WACE and F. H. STUBBINGS (eds.), *A Companion to Homer*. London: Macmillan, 1962, pp. 179–214.

———— "Homer's Originality: Oral Dictated Texts," *Transactions and Proceedings of the American Philological Association*, LXXXIV (1953), 124–34.

———— "The Poetics of Oral Creation," in W. P. Friederich (ed.), *Comparative Literature*. ("Proceedings of the Second Congress of the International Comparative Literature Association, 1958.") Chapel Hill: University of North Carolina Press, 1959, vol. I, pp. 1–6.

———— (ed.). *Serbocroatian Heroic Songs. Vol. I: Novi Pazar: English Translations*. Collected by MILMAN PARRY and edited and translated by A. B. LORD. Cambridge: Harvard University Press, 1954.

———— *The Singer of Tales*. ("Harvard Studies in Comparative Literature," no. 24.) Cambridge: Harvard University Press, 1960.

MAGOUN, F. P., JR. "Bede's Story of Caedmon: The Case History of an Anglo-Saxon Oral Singer," *Speculum*, XXX (1955), 49–63.

———— "Oral-Formulaic Character of Anglo-Saxon Narrative Poetry," *Speculum*, XXVIII (1953), 446–67.

———— "The Theme of the Beasts of Battle in Anglo-Saxon Poetry," *Neuphilologische Mitteilungen*, LVI (1955), 81–89.

MCLEOD, W. E. "Oral Bards at Delphi," *Transactions and Proceedings of the American Philological Association*, XCII (1961), 317–25.

MOWINCKEL, S. *Psalmenstudien II: Das Thronbesteigungsfest Jahwäs und der Ursprung der Eschatologie*. ("Videnskapsselskapets Skrifter, II, Hist-Filos. Klasse," 1921, no. 6.) Kristiania: Jacob Dybwad, 1922.

—————— *Psalmenstudien VI: Die Psalmdichter.* ("Videnskapsselskapets Skrifter, II, Hist-Filos. Klasse," 1924, no. 1.) Kristiania: Jacob Dybwad, 1924.

—————— *The Psalms in Israel's Worship.* Translated by D. R. Ap-Thomas. 2 vols.; Oxford: Blackwell, 1962.

MUSIL, A. *Arabia Petraea.* Vol. III. Vienna: Alfred Hoelder, 1908.

—————— *The Manners and Customs of the Rwala Bedouins.* New York: American Geographical Society, 1928.

NICHOLS, S. G., JR. *Formulaic Diction and Thematic Composition in the Chanson de Roland.* ("University of North Carolina Studies in the Romance Languages and Literatures," no. 36.) Chapel Hill: University of North Carolina Press, 1961.

NIELSEN, E. *Oral Tradition.* ("Studies in Biblical Theology," no. 11.) London: S.C.M. Press, 1954.

NOTH, M. *Das System der Zwölf Stämme Israels.* ("Beiträge zur Wissenschaft vom Alten und Neuen Testament," IV. Folge, Heft 1.) Stuttgart: W. Kohlhammer, 1930.

NOTOPOULOS, J. A. "Continuity and Interconnexion in Homeric Oral Composition," *Transactions and Proceedings of the American Philological Association,* LXXXII (1951), 81–101.

—————— "Homer, Hesiod and the Achaean Heritage of Oral Poetry," *Hesperia,* XXIX (1960), 177–97.

—————— "The Homeric Hymns as Oral Poetry: A Study of Post Homeric Oral Tradition," *American Journal of Philology,* LXXXIII (1962), 337–68.

—————— "Studies in Early Greek Poetry," *Harvard Studies in Classical Philology,* LXVIII (1964), 1–77.

NYBERG, N. S. *Studien zum Hoseabuche.* "Uppsala Universitets Årsskrift," 1935:6.

O'NEIL, W. A. "Another Look at Oral Poetry in *The Seafarer,*" *Speculum,* XXXV (1960), 596–600.

PARRY, M. "Studies in the Epic Technique of Oral Verse-Making. I: Homer and Homeric Style," *Harvard Studies in Classical Philology,* XLI (1930), 73–147.

—————— "Studies in the Epic Technique of Oral Verse-Making. II: the Homeric Language as the Language of an Oral Poetry," *Harvard Studies in Classical Philology,* XLIII (1932), 1–50.

—————— "Whole Formulaic Verses in Greek and Southslavic Heroic Songs," *Transactions and Proceedings of the American Philological Association,* LXIV (1933), 179–97.

PATTON, J. H. *Canaanite Parallels in the Book of Psalms.* Baltimore: Johns Hopkins Press, 1944.

VAN DER PLOEG, J. "Le rôle de la tradition orale dans la transmission du texte de l'Ancien Testament," *Revue Biblique,* LIV (1947), 5–41.

PODECHARD, E. *Le Psautier I: Traduction littérale et explication historique.* ("Bibliothèque de la Faculté Catholique de Théologie de Lyon," vol. 3.) Lyon: Faculté Catholique, 1949.

REVELL, E. J. "The Order of the Elements in the Verbal Statement Clause in 1Q Serek," *Revue de Qumran,* III (1962), 559–69.

—————— "A Structural Analysis of the Grammar of the 'Manual of Discipline'

(1QS)." An unpublished thesis for the degree of Doctor of Philosophy at the University of Toronto, 1962.

Ross, J. "Formulaic Composition in Gaelic Oral Literature," *Modern Philology*, LVII (1959), 1–12.

Rychner, J. "La chanson de geste, épopée vivante," *La Table Ronde*, CXXXII (1958), 152–67.

Schmaus, A. "Formel und metrisch-syntaktisches Modell," *Die Welt der Slaven*, V (1960), 395–408.

Sharma, R. K. *Elements of Poetry in the Mahābhārata*. ("University of California Publications in Classical Philology," vol. 20.) Berkeley: University of California Press, 1964.

Skendi, S. *Albanian and South Slavic Oral Epic Poetry*. ("Memoirs of the American Folklore Society," vol. 44.) Philadelphia: American Folklore Society, 1954.

Sokolov, Y. M. *Russian Folklore*. Translated by C. R. Smith. New York: Macmillan, 1950.

Thurnwald, R. C. *Profane Literature of the Buin, Solomon Islands*. ("Yale University Publications in Anthropology," no. 8.) New Haven, 1936.

Tsevat, M. *A Study of the Language of the Biblical Psalms*. ("Journal of Biblical Literature Monograph Series," vol. 9.) Philadelphia, 1955.

Waldron, R. A. "Oral-Formulaic Technique and Middle English Alliterative Poetry," *Speculum*, XXXII (1957), 792–804.

Weiser, A. *Die Psalmen. Das Alte Testament Deutsch*. 6th ed.; Göttingen: Vandenhoeck & Ruprecht, 1963.

Wente, E. E. "Egyptian 'Make Merry' Songs Reconsidered," *Journal of Near Eastern Studies*, XXI (1962), 118–28.

Wevers, J. W. "Semitic Bound Structures," *Canadian Journal of Linguistics*, VII (1961), 9–13.

———— "A Study in the Form Criticism of Individual Complaint Psalms," *Vetus Testamentum*, VI (1956), 80–96.

Whallon, W. "Formulaic Poetry in the Old Testament," *Comparative Literature*, XV (1963), 1–14.

Whitman, C. H. *Homer and the Heroic Tradition*. Cambridge: Harvard University Press, 1958.

Winner, T. G. *The Oral Art and Literature of the Kazakhs of Russian Central Asia*. Durham: Duke University Press, 1958.

Index

Printed in Belgium